Impact VALUES

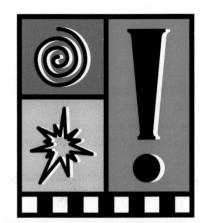

30 DISCUSSION TOPICS TO HELP YOU EXPLORE YOUR OWN VALUES

Richard R. Day
Junko Yamanaka
Joseph Shaules

Series Editor
Michael Rost

Longman

Published by
Longman Asia ELT
2/F Cornwall House
Taikoo Place
979 King's Road
Quarry Bay
Hong Kong

fax: +852 2856 9578
e-mail: aelt@pearsoned.com.hk
www.longman.com

and Associated Companies throughout the world.

© Pearson Education North Asia Limited 2003

This book was developed for Longman Asia ELT by Lateral Communications Limited, USA.

First published 2003
Produced by Pearson Education North Asia Limited, Hong Kong

Series Editor: Michael Rost
Project Editor: Ruth Desmond
Art Director: Keiko Kimura
Cover Design: Keiko Kimura
Recording Engineer: Glenn.Davidson

Recording Credits: Ellen Schwartz, Rick Tabor, Cassidy Brown, Rachel Peters, Marvin Greene, Scott Grinthal, Scot Crisp, Rami Margron, Katie Demps, Katie Hemmeter, John Hull, Jerry Lawrence, Carrie Francis, Keiko Nakamura, Natalia Bartolotti, Brad Lucido, Hyonchol Park, Kaitlin Friedman, Wayne Lee, Henry Stoltenberg, Stephanie Wagner, Steven Thomas, Daniel Kim, Amy Parker

Photo Credits: PhotoDisc Ltd., Keiko Kimura, Ammon Rost

ISBN 962 00 5263 3

Acknowledgements

The authors and publishers would like to thank the following people who participated in the surveys, reviews, and piloting stages of *Impact Values*. We greatly appreciate your input and collaboration on this project.

Keith Adams
Fiona Bolton
Hui Olivia Chang
Derek Pi-hua Chu
Robert Croker
Brenda Cunliffe
Brad Deacon
C. A. Edington
Raji Fernando
James Goddard
Lynda Gomi
Louise Haynes
Yu-chen Hsu
Gretchen Jude
Fuyuko Kato

Hsui-Yun Bonnie Liao
Yow-Yu Brian Lin
Jonathan Lynch
Chun-chi Jolene Mao
Daniel Minor
Ian Platt
William B. Porter
Nevitt Reagan
Andrew Reimann
Mark D. Sheehan
Tony Silva
Debbie Waselyshen
James Welker
Matthew White
Kathryn Zidonis

Special appreciation goes to Takanori Niinomi and Midori Yamanaka for their inspiration.

Introduction

Impact Values will help you express your ideas in English and understand other people's ideas better. You can use this book by yourself or you can use it in class with other students.

HOW TO USE *IMPACT VALUES* BY YOURSELF:

The best way to begin is with the Intro Unit. This unit shows you how to use each of the 30 units in the book.
❶ Read the instructions for each of the activities and then try each activity.

❷ Next, look at the Contents. There are five major themes or categories: People; Relationships; Workplace; Family; and Society. Each category has six topics that explore important values in our lives.

This book is different from other books — you do not have to go from the beginning to the end. You can start with any category or topic that you want to. Which category do you like most? Pick one category. Then study the six topics. Start with one that you really like.

❸ Now go to the topic. Go through each activity just as you did in the Intro Unit. Begin with Warm Up. Listen to the audio CD while you read along. Read and listen two or three times. (The Situations are all recorded in natural settings, so you will hear very natural English with natural background sounds on the CD.) Then try the Check Your Understanding questions to make sure you understand the topic.

❹ After you understand the topic, study the Points of View section carefully. Think about the opinions and the supporting statements. Match the supporting statements to the opinions. Then decide: Do you agree with the three people? Why or why not? Write or say your opinion. Then think about your views for What Are Your Values? Write your own opinion and reasons. Take your time and do each step carefully. This way, you'll learn more.

> If you have a friend who is learning English, try to use this book together. It's fun to compare your ideas and opinions with another person. If you use the book with a friend, you might try to do the discussion activity at the end of each unit.

HOW TO USE *IMPACT VALUES* IN CLASS:

WARM UP
In this activity, you will answer three or four questions about the topic of the unit. Work with a classmate.
❶ Ask each other the questions and compare your answers. After you finish, you will have some clear ideas about your own beliefs.

SITUATION
The Situation tells you a short story about the topic. It shows you the values and beliefs of the people in the story.
❷ Read the story or listen to it on CD while you read. The Situations are all recorded in natural settings, so you will have the chance to hear very natural English with natural background sounds. Each story has some numbered words and expressions (like this[1]). You can look these up in the Glossary at the back of the book.

> After you have finished, you should feel that you understand the people's values in the story. You should be able to answer these questions: What do they believe? Why do they believe that? Don't try to say if you agree or not at this time. Just try to understand their values.

If you don't understand the main ideas of the story, read or listen again. Or ask your teacher or classmates for help.

CHECK YOUR UNDERSTANDING
❸ Now you will answer two or three questions. The questions will help you understand the story better.

POINTS OF VIEW

This activity has two parts: Opinions and Supporting Statements. The opinion section show you three opinions by three people. These are different "points of view" – different ways of looking at the topic. The Supporting Statements section shows you six ideas that "support" the opinions or show the reasons why someone has an opinion.

❹ Read each supporting statement and think about which opinion it *supports the most*. Write the number of each supporting statement under the opinion that it fits best.

This section will help you develop your thinking skills in English. It will help you understand different opinions and help you connect opinions and reasons.

❺ When you finish, compare your answers with a classmate. Do you have the same answers? Why or why not?

❻ The next step is: Work in a group of three. Ask your partners: Do you agree with Person 1? with Person 2? with Person 3? For each person, say if you "really agree," "agree," "disagree," or "really disagree."

WHAT ARE YOUR VALUES?

This activity is very challenging, but it is also a lot of fun! It will help you express your own opinion and explain your supporting reasons.

❼ The first step is expressing your position. Think about the Situation. Write your "position" or your "advice" in the box on the left. Be sure it is clear. Then write your supporting reasons in the box on the right. You can use ideas from the Points of View section and add your original ideas.

❽ The second step is Clarifying. Stand up. Walk around the classroom. Ask your classmates, "What is your position?" or "What do you think of this topic?" Take about 5 to 10 minutes to talk to several classmates. When you find two class-mates with *similar positions*, sit together.

Now compare your reasons with the other classmates in your group. Make a list of all of your reasons. Rank the reasons in order: #1 is the most important reason, #2 is next most important, and so on. In your group, practice what you will say to classmates who do not agree with your opinion. (For example, "If someone says..., what should we say?") Spend about 5 or 10 minutes practicing together.

❾ The third step is Exchanging. Form a group with classmates who have *different positions* on the topic. Present your position and your reasons to the group. Listen carefully to their positions and reasons. Ask questions to understand their supporting reasons better. (For example, "Why do you think that?" "What is your reason for believing that?") After everyone has spoken and answered questions, take a vote in your group: Who has the strongest position and supporting reasons? That person "wins" the debate.

After you have finished this activity, you should understand your classmates' opinions and their supporting reasons. You should also have a clearer idea of your own opinion and supporting reasons. You may even have changed your mind.

DISCUSSION ACTIVITY

❿ The final activity in each unit is different. It might be a discussion or an exchange, a role play, a survey, a debate, or a personal story. Follow the instructions for the activity and have fun!

To the Teacher

Impact Values is a complete course in oral communication for students who already have fundamental speaking, listening, reading, and writing skills in English. *Impact Values* is based on a collection of 30 current topics that adult students have expressed an interest in discussing. The topics are organized into five categories or themes, and each topic is carefully presented with exercises to help students understand the topics and express their own ideas and values.

Here is an overview of the eight activities in each unit.

Warm up
❶ This activity introduces the topic. Have your students answer the questions individually. Then you can have them compare their responses with a classmate. This activity should take about 3 to 5 minutes. The purpose of the activity is to make sure the students are thinking about their own opinions and are getting comfortable talking to each other.

Situation
> The situation tells a short story about the topic. It presents the values of the people in the story, through a dialogue or monologue. There is a short introduction followed by one or two general questions.

❷ Tell your students to think about the questions as they read the story. You can have the students read the story and listen to it on the CD at the same time, or you can have them read it without listening to the CD. If you do this, you might have them read the story a second time, and also listen to the CD as they read. (You can also assign students to listen to the CD as homework to preview or review a topic.)

> Note that the monologues and dialogues are all recorded in natural settings (like homes or offices), with natural sound effects, so that the students have an opportunity to hear more "authentic" spoken English.

❸ When your students have finished, ask for answers to the questions. The point of these questions is to make sure the students have a general understanding of the situation and the values presented. Depending on the length of the story, and how many times the students read and listen to the story, this activity could take from 5 to 10 minutes.

Check your understanding
❹ There are several questions about the story to help students understand it. You might tell your students to answer each question and then compare their answers with a classmate. If you like, you can lead a brief discussion on the story, to be sure that everyone understands the points of view of each person in the story.

> After they have answered and discussed the questions, your students should have a good understanding of the story and the people's values. If not, you might want to go back and have them read the story again, and listen to the story on the CD, or give them a short synopsis of the story in different words. Some words and expressions in the stories are annotated with a superscript (like this[1]) . These words and expressions are in the Glossary in the back of the book.

Points of view
❺ This section shows three people who have different *Opinions* about the topic. Instruct your students to read their opinions and to think about them. Next, look at the *Supporting Statements*. These are six reasons or claims that support the opinions. There are two supporting statements for each opinion. Tell your students to find two supporting statements for each opinion and write the numbers of the statements in the boxes below each opinion. Often a supporting statement can be associated with more than one opinion, so ask the students to think carefully to find the statements that *best* support each opinion.

❻ Then have the students work in groups of three to compare their answers. Regrouping students often is helpful in teaching *Impact Values* because it allows the students to hear the opinions and ideas of several different students in their class. It may also help them develop their confidence and enthusiasm for expressing their ideas and understanding the ideas of others.

❼ After the students have spent 5 to 10 minutes on this activity, you might want to check your students' responses. Discuss the cases in which some supporting statements seem to support more than one opinion. In cases where students have chosen three supporting statements for a single opinion, tell them to select one of the three statements that could *also* support another opinion. Also emphasize that in the realm of opinions and supporting claims, there is not always one right answer! (An answer key for this section is provided in the Teacher Support material, available at www.impactseries.com/values)

❽ Finally, tell the students to ask each other about their reactions to the opinions of the three people. They will ask each other if they agree with each of the three people (e.g., *Do you agree with Trin?*). The partners will respond, expressing their agreement (e.g., *Yes, I agree with Trin*) or disagreement (e.g., *No, I don't agree with Trin*).
When your students have finished this section, they should have a good understanding of different points of view about the topic. This is an important preparation step for the next section.

What are your values?
❾ This section asks students for their opinions about the topic or advice for the people in the story. Allow each student a few minutes to express their position and supporting reasons clearly. They can write in the boxes in the book, or on a separate sheet of paper.

Clarifying and exchanging
❿ This section gives students a chance to further develop their ideas and opinions and communicate them to their classmates.

- Clarifying

This activity requires students to stand up and move around the classroom to find two classmates who have the same or a similar answer to the question in What Are Your Values? When a student finds two classmates with the same or a similar answer, instruct the three of them to sit together. Their task is to compare their reasons and to make a list of all of the reasons that the three of them have. If they want to, they can add new ones. When they have done this, instruct them to rank their reasons, with #1 being the strongest, and so on.

Finally, the students in each group should practice what they will say to classmates who do not agree with their position. This prepares them for the next activity, Exchanging. Encourage the students to think about alternate points of view and to rehearse their responses to people who have different points of view.

As your students do this activity, check each group's position or advice. You will need this information in order to place students in different groups in the next activity.

- Exchanging

The purpose of this activity is for students to exchange their values or opinions with students who have different values or opinions. Place students in groups so that a full range of different answers or positions is represented. Tell the students to present their positions and their reasons. The students will try to explain to the other members of their group, who hold different positions, why they believe in their answers or positions. Remind your students to ask each other questions if something is not clear, or if they need to know more about the person's reasons.

After 10 or 15 minutes, tell the students to take a vote in their groups. They should vote for the strongest position and supporting reasons. One way to close or finish the activity is to ask each group to present the results of the vote.

Communication activity
Each chapter ends with a communication activity. This activity expands on the topic of the unit and requires students to use the information they learned from the previous activities.

Follow-up activities
There are a number of follow-up activities you can try if you wish to extend any of the units in class, or if you wish to assign students homework activities. See the Appendix: Extension Activities for ideas, or visit www.impactseries.com/values

Timing of a unit
Teaching one unit can take from 45 to 75 minutes, depending on the English ability of the students, and how long you want to spend on each activity. When you have finished the last activity, you can either pick a new topic in the same category, or select a new category and a new topic.

WAYS OF USING THE BOOK

There are many ways that you can use the material in this book to help your students improve their reading and their listening and speaking abilities in English. Here is one option:

❶ Begin with the Intro Unit, Talking about Your Values. This unit explains how to do each of the activities. We suggest that you look it over carefully before using it in class. Then in class, work through the unit. Make sure that your students understand how to do each activity.

❷ You might want to keep a record of your students' responses to the communication activity, which asks them to select the topics in the book that are most interesting to them. You can use that information to help you decide which units to cover.

> This book is different from other books — you do not have to work from the beginning to the end of the book. You can start with any of the categories or topics that you or your students want to, and move around the book as you wish.

❸ Finally, there are many other activities that you can do as follow up work once the students have finished the unit. For example:

• Give the students a written assignment on the topic. They can do research from outside sources, including web resources at www.impactseries.com/values, and bring printouts to class to share with other students.

• Have a mini-debate: First, make a statement of the topic. (For example, for unit 10: The Computer Nut, you can make this debate statement: Computers can hurt a relationship.) Then divide the class into groups of six or eight. Have two or three students argue for the debate statement, have two or three argue against it, and have one or two students "judge" and choose the winning side.

We hope that your students and you will enjoy using this book. Please let us us know your comments and suggestions. We would enjoy hearing from you. Please visit www.impactseries.com/values for more teaching support and to exchange ideas.

Contents

Talking about Your Values

WARM UP

1. Do you like learning English?

2. Why do people learn English?

3. Why are you learning English?

4. What's the hardest part of learning English for you?

1. You can think about your answers or write them down. Take about 3 minutes.
2. Now, work with a classmate. Ask each other the questions and compare your answers.

1. Read the Situation introduction and look at the question.
2. Now, read the story and listen to it on the CD at the same time. Think about the question as you read and listen.
3. Discuss the questions with your classmates and teacher.
4. If you are having trouble, read the story and listen to the CD again.

The numbered words are in the glossary on pages 82-88. If you don't know these words, you can look them up.

SITUATION

∩ **Richard, Junko, and Joseph are writing Impact Values. Do they agree about the topics that will be used in the book?**

Richard: In my opinion, *Impact Values* needs to have a lot of topics about students' personal beliefs. When students investigate[1] their personal beliefs in English, they learn better.

Junko: Well, some students may learn better, but I know some students are reluctant[2] to talk to each other about personal experiences. I believe that *Impact Values* should teach students to use English to discuss important global topics[3].

Joseph: My idea is a little different. I think *Impact Values* should stress cross-cultural communication[4]. Students learn English best when they're talking about their own culture.

CHECK YOUR UNDERSTANDING

1. What does Richard believe are the best topics?

....

2. Does Junko agree with Richard?

....

3. What is Joseph's idea?

....

1. Answer each question.
2. Compare your answers with a classmate.

1. Read the opinions and think about them.
2. Then look at the Supporting Statements. Find two supporting statements for each opinion. Write the number of the Supporting Statements that match the opinion in the boxes.
3. Compare your answers with your class-mate's. Ask your teacher if you need help.

POINTS OF VIEW Read these three opinions.

Trin

We can learn English without expressing our opinions. ☐1 ☐4

Monica

I want to talk about my culture with people from other countries. ☐3 ☐5 ☐2 ☐6

Koji

Talking about global issues is a waste of time.

Match the supporting statements with the opinions. Write the numbers in the boxes. Each opinion has two supporting statements.

supporting statements

1

Personal opinions are private.

2

English class is for learning English, not world topics.

3

English is an international language that belongs to everyone who speaks it.

4

The opinions of students are not important.

5

Learning about other cultures and ways of thinking is interesting.

6

Discussing personal beliefs in class is too emotional for me.

Now compare with a classmate.

1. Write your advice in the first box.
2. Now write your reasons in the second box. You can think for a few minutes before you write. Try to write at least two new reasons.

Work in a group of three. Ask your partners:
Do you agree with Trin? Do you agree with Monica?
Do you agree with Koji?
Answer for each person: *I really agree / I agree /*
I disagree / I really disagree.

STEP 1: CLARIFYING (Spend about 10-15 minutes doing this step.)
1. Look at your advice in WHAT ARE YOUR VALUES?
2. Walk around the room. Ask your class-mates about their advice.
3. When you find two classmates with similar advice, sit together.
4. Now compare your reasons. Next, make a list of all of your reasons. If you want to, add new ones.
5. Now rank the reasons. #1 is the strongest, #2 is the next strongest, and so on.
6. In your group, practice what you will say to classmates who do not agree with your advice.

STEP 2: EXCHANGING (Spend about 10-15 minutes doing this step.)
1. Your teacher will put you in a group that has different advice and reasons.
2. Present your advice and your reasons to the group. Try to explain why your advice is better.
3. When you listen to other group members, ask questions if their reasons are not clear.
4. Take a vote in your group: Which advice is the best?

WHAT ARE YOUR VALUES?

What advice would you give Richard, Junko, and Joseph about writing Impact Values? What are your reasons?

Advice → Reasons →

CLARIFYING & EXCHANGING

Now form groups and discuss your advice and reasons.

Follow the instructions and have fun!

COMMUNICATION ACTIVITY

Work with a classmate. Study the Table of Contents (pages 8-9).
Place the topics in three categories: Personal Opinion, Global Issues,
Cross-Cultural Communication. Which of these are the most interesting for you?
For your partner?

VALUES of PEOPLE

In this section you'll learn about some of the different personal choices people make, and why.

1 Pierced

刺穿 突破
[iə]

How do you decorate yourself? Is it okay to pierce your body?

A young man gives his opinion about his girlfriend's piercings.

2 TV or Not TV?

Is TV a positive or a negative influence in your life?

Is it possible to watch too much TV?

A woman talks about the effect TV has had on her life.

3 Beautiful Men

What kind of person do you consider beautiful?

Does makeup make someone more or less beautiful to you?

Four friends share their ideas about makeup and beauty.

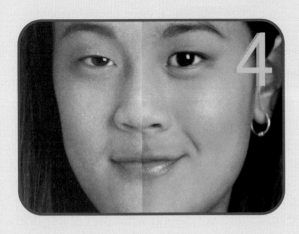

4 Cosmetic Surgery

Is it okay to change your natural appearance?

Why do some people want to change their appearance through surgery?

A young woman discusses her plan for getting cosmetic surgery.

5 I Can't Say No

How much should we help our friends and family?

How much should we help people we don't know very well?

One man wonders if he's helping people too much.

6 Embarrassing Mother!

Is it okay for people to dress any way they want?

Should people always "act their age"?

A teenager talks about her mother's desire to look and act young.

VALUES of PEOPLE

Pierced

WARM UP
1. What do you think of piercing?
2. Do you have any piercings? Would you like to get some?
3. Do any of your friends have parts of their bodies pierced (ears, nose)?

SITUATION 🎧 Phil is talking with his friend Brian. Phil is unhappy with his girlfriend, Michelle. Why is he unhappy?

Brian: So, how's Michelle? You guys are still going out together?

Phil: Yeah, we are, but, I don't know. It's actually getting kind of weird[1]. I'm not sure it's going to last.

Brian: Are you serious? Man, you've got to find a way to make it last[2]. Michelle is awesome[3]! She's got everything!

Phil: Yeah, she is great. Really energetic —

Brian: Yeah!

Phil: And fun to be with, and... But, this is going to sound stupid.

Brian: What?

Phil: It's her piercings.

Brian: Yeah, so, what about them?

Phil: Well, first she got her nose pierced.

Brian: Cool[4].

Phil: And then her belly button[5].

Brian: Her belly button? Wow. I didn't know she did that.

Phil: I guess that was okay.

Brian: Yeah!

Phil: But then she went and got her tongue pierced. I don't know if I can deal with it.

Brian: Tongue piercing? Have you kissed her yet?

Phil: Yeah, I did kiss her!

Brian: Cool, huh?

Phil: It was disgusting[6]!

Brian: Disgusting?

Phil: It felt dirty! And now every time I think about it I just start wondering what part of her body she's going to pierce next.

Brian: Well, have you told her how you feel about it?

Phil: Yeah, I tried.

Brian: And?

Phil: I asked her if she could stop wearing some of them, at least when we were together.

Brian: What did she say about that?

Phil: She said it was her right to express herself[7]. You know, she said something like, "Look, you can't control the way I look. You should accept me the way I am." I was, like, what?

Brian: I don't know, man, I think you just don't get it. You can't let a few pieces of metal get between you and the woman of your dreams.

Phil: Well, I don't know if she's the woman of my dreams anymore.

Brian: What?

Phil: Besides, now every time when we get together she tells me how good I'd look with pierced ears. It's bad enough that she's getting pierced. Now she wants me to do it, too?

Brian: Why not, man? It's no big deal. And, you know, if it turns Michelle on[8]...

Phil: I can't believe you agree with her.

Brian: Totally[9].

Phil: I don't know what I'm going to do.

Brian: You're going to get a piercing, man!

CHECK YOUR UNDERSTANDING

1. How does Phil feel about Michelle's piercings?

....

2. What does Brian think about them?

....

3. What does Michelle want Phil to do?

....

Read these three opinions.

Amber

If Phil really loves her, he will get used to her body piercing.

Anton

If Michelle really loves Phil, she will stop wearing her piercings.

Monica

Body piercing is neither natural nor beautiful.

Match the supporting statements with the opinions. Write the numbers in the boxes.
Each opinion has two supporting statements.

supporting statements

1

True love is deeper than physical beauty.

2

In any relationship, people have to be understanding.

3

We were born without holes in our bodies.

4

Our bodies are gifts that we should not change or damage.

5

Phil needs to be patient. People can get used to almost anything.

6

Michelle should not be overly concerned about fashion.

Now compare with a classmate.

Work in a group of three. Ask your partners:
Do you agree with Amber? Do you agree with Anton? Do you agree with Monica?
Answer for each person: *I really agree / I agree / I disagree / I really disagree.*

WHAT ARE YOUR VALUES?

How should Phil and Michelle solve their problem? Write your advice and your reasons.
Use new ideas in addition to the ideas above.

Advice

Reasons

CLARIFYING & EXCHANGING

Now form groups and discuss your advice and reasons.

OPINION EXCHANGE

What would you do for fashion? Fill out the chart. Work with a partner. Talk about each idea.

- pierce my _____
  (part of body)

- wear a (an) _____
  (item of clothing)

- get a tattoo of _____ on my _____
  (something)   (part of body)

- use _____
  (kind / color of makeup)

- dye my hair _____
  (color)

- your idea _____

1

VALUES of PEOPLE

TV or Not TV?

WARM UP
1. How much television do you watch? (None / Hardly any/ 1–2 hours a day/ 3–4 hours a day)
2. Why do you watch television?
3. What programs do you like?

SITUATION ∩ Leah is talking about her time as a college student. Why did she decide to stop watching television?

My family loves television. My earliest memories are of watching TV with my family. I think we had five or six television sets at home—the bedrooms, the kitchen, everywhere! At least one television was on all of the time.

When I went to university, I lived in a dormitory[1] my first year. Of course I had a TV, so I continued watching my favorite programs. But after a while, I realized I had a problem. My courses were hard — much harder than high school — and there was a lot of homework. Also, I felt stressed in my new environment. I started watching more TV to help me relax. Guess what? Soon I was spending more time watching TV than I was on homework. Plus, I didn't have a lot of friends. Maybe a childhood full of television made me less social[2]. At the end of my first year, my grades weren't very good, and I was really disappointed in myself.

At home that summer, I watched television with my family a lot. At first I thought it was great. But then I noticed something. We talked all the time, but...always about TV. Something was missing. Television brought us together, but in a way it also kept us apart.

When I got back to university, I made up my mind[3] to do better. I walked into my dormitory, and started to turn the TV on. But then an idea popped into my head[4]: "Stop watching TV!" Suddenly it became crystal clear[5]: my old friend television was really my enemy! It had kept me from getting good grades, and from making friends. I had to stop watching TV.

I did. I quit. I gave away my television, and I've never looked back. I started doing better in school, made more friends, actually started having more energy.

I don't know if I'll continue to lead a TV-free life. But if I do watch television again, it won't be like before. I have vowed[6] that television will never again be a major part of my life.

1. What role does TV play in Leah's family? ....
2. Why did Leah stop watching TV? ....
3. What happened after Leah stopped watching TV? ....

POINTS OF VIEW

Read these three opinions.

James

Trin

Pablo

Our lives would be better if we didn't watch TV.

It is okay to watch some TV, but not too much.

Television is an important part of our lives.

Match the supporting statements with the opinions. Write the numbers in the boxes.
Each opinion has two supporting statements.

supporting statements

1

Watching television takes the place of more important things in life.

2

Television is a major source of news, information, and pleasure.

3

Some TV programs are valuable, but some are a waste of time.

4

When people watch a lot of television, they gain weight.

5

Sometimes we need entertainment.

6

Television is a good form of entertainment.

Now compare with a classmate.

Work in a group of three. Ask your partners:
Do you agree with James? Do you agree with Trin? Do you agree with Pablo?
Answer for each person: *I really agree / I agree / I disagree / I really disagree.*

WHAT ARE YOUR VALUES?

Should Leah start watching television again? State your position and support your ideas.
Use new ideas in addition to the ideas above.

Your Position ➤ Supporting Statements ➤

CLARIFYING & EXCHANGING

Now form groups and discuss your position and supporting statements.

VALUES PROJECT

Work with a partner. Find out what your classmates think about television. Make about 10 questions.

1. ....
2. ....
3. ....
4. ....
5. ....

6. ....
7. ....
8. ....
9. ....
10. ....

example
1. I like to watch television. True? False?
2. Why do you watch television?
3. What is your favorite program?

Ask your classmates and your teacher your questions. Write their answers.
Analyze your results and write a short report. Share the results with the class.

3 Beautiful Men

WARM UP

1. Is beauty important to you? For yourself? For other people?

2. Do you like to be called "beautiful"?

3. Can you name some "beautiful" male singers? Actors? TV personalities?

SITUATION **Yumi and Amani have just started dating. They're talking about each other to their friends. What is Amani like? What is Yumi like?**

Yumi: I'm so glad you finally got a chance to meet Amani, because I think I'm falling in love with him.

Sara: Wow!

Yumi: What did you think of him?

Sara: Come on. You can't really be serious about a guy who wears makeup?

Yumi: Why not? I mean, he's beautiful, and... and I think that men should be beautiful if they want to.

Sara: But it's just not natural, you know? I — okay — he was beautiful, and... I don't know if I prefer a guy looking beautiful. Maybe more, you know, naturally good-looking. Rugged[1], masculine[2].

Yumi: Why? I mean, you wear makeup. Look at you: you've got on foundation[3] and blush[4].

Sara: I know.

Yumi: And how long did you spend on your hair this morning?

Sara: Well, an hour. But, okay — that's not the point. I'm a woman. Women wear makeup. Women spend an hour on their hair in the morning. It's just — that's how it is. It's totally different.

Yumi: And who came up with these social stereotypes[5]? Why can't men look beautiful if they want to?

Amani: I'm so glad you finally got to meet Yumi, because I think I'm falling in love with her.

George: Amani, she doesn't wear any makeup.

Amani: Well, no, She doesn't wear makeup, but that's okay.

George: Doesn't that seem weird[6] to you?

Amani: No. What's wrong with that? There's no problem with her not wearing makeup. She looks so beautiful without that...

George: Well, wouldn't she be, then, more beautiful if she were to wear makeup? I mean, it's not a question of whether she needs it or not... doesn't it just strike[7] you as a little...

Amani: Well...

George: ...odd that she doesn't wear makeup?

Amani: Well, I mean, why should she be forced to wear makeup, really, when you think about it? I mean, she doesn't need it.

George: Because that's what women do.

Amani: Oh, but who came up with these social stereotypes? Why do women have to wear makeup to be considered beautiful?

CHECK YOUR UNDERSTANDING

1. Describe Yumi's boyfriend. ....

2. What is Sara's view about men who wear makeup? ....

3. What is Amani's view of women who don't wear makeup?...................................

POINTS OF VIEW

Read these three opinions.

Carmen

It is okay for men to wear makeup.

Anton

Makeup is for women. It is wrong for men to wear makeup.

Monica

No one (men or women) should care too much about how they look.

Match the supporting statements with the opinions. Write the numbers in the boxes. Each opinion has two supporting statements.

supporting statements

1
Men should look masculine, not beautiful.

2
Men and women should not spend too much time and money on cosmetics. Natural is best.

3
Men are behaving too much like women these days.

4
People often judge others by their looks. So men should make every effort to look neat, too.

5
It is important for young men to be nice-looking to attract women.

6
Inner beauty is more important than looks. Use your time and money for getting skills or knowledge, rather than on cosmetics.

Now compare with a classmate.

Work in a group of three. Ask your partners:
Do you agree with Carmen? Do you agree with Anton? Do you agree with Monica?
Answer for each person: *I really agree / I agree / I disagree / I really disagree.*

WHAT ARE YOUR VALUES?

Is it okay for men to wear makeup? State your position and support your ideas.
Use new ideas in addition to the ideas above.

Your Position → Supporting Statements →

CLARIFYING & EXCHANGING

Now form groups and discuss your position and supporting statements.

VALUES SURVEY

What "beauty care" activities are okay? Make a check for each activity. Do it quickly. Don't think too long!

	Okay for women only	Okay for both men and women	Depends on ____
wearing lipstick	....	....	....
shaving legs	....	....	....
shaping eyebrows	....	....	....
having long hair	....	....	....
wearing foundation	....	....	....

	Okay for women only	Okay for both men and women	Depends on ____
getting pedicures	....	....	....
wearing earrings	....	....	....
applying face pack	....	....	....
add your own ideas:	....	....	....

Compare answers with a partner. Then, compare answers as a class.

Cosmetic Surgery

WARM UP

1. How important are "good looks" to you?

2. What do you do to "look good"?

3. Would you ever consider having cosmetic surgery? Why or why not?

SITUATION 🎧 **Ayu is 18 years old. She wants to have cosmetic surgery on her face. What does she want to change? Why? What does her mother think?**

Ayu: Mom, I have something exciting to tell you.

Mother: What's up?

Ayu: I'm going to have an operation to get my eyelids fixed[1].

Mother: What? Are you saying that you're going to get cosmetic surgery[2]? At a hospital?

Ayu: Well, it's... it's not so expensive, and it's only my eyelids.

Mother: Only your eyelids?!

Ayu: Yeah. It's not like I'm going to, you know, do anything drastic[3]. I'm just going to fix it so I can look prettier. And Mom, it's my money. I've saved it. I've been working to save my money, and I... it's my body.

Mother: So that explains it. That's why you've been working all those jobs. You're beautiful the way you are. You look great.

Ayu: But, Mom, boys don't see what you see in me. If I look beautiful, then, you know, I'll be approached[4] by more boys. Maybe I'll have a chance to get jobs that I wouldn't be able to if I didn't fix my eyelids.

Mother: Honey, you should attract[5] people with your inner beauty. Your personality, your intelligence — not your looks.

Ayu: Mom, you don't understand. Boys aren't attracted by your intelligence and your wit[6]. The first thing they see is your looks. If you're not beautiful, they won't approach you at all. Then how are they to know if you have wit or intelligence?

Mother: You can't do this.

Ayu: Mom, I'm doing it whether you like it or not.

Mother: I think you're making a terrible mistake.

before

after

CHECK YOUR UNDERSTANDING

1. What is Ayu's idea about beauty? Is it the same as her mother's idea?

....

2. How is Ayu going to pay for her cosmetic surgery?

....

3. Will Ayu take her mother's advice?

....

Read these three opinions.

Pablo

Ayu should have the cosmetic surgery now.

Ray

Ayu should think more about it and decide later.

Amber

Ayu should not have the surgery.

Match the supporting statements with the opinions. Write the numbers in the boxes.
Each opinion has two supporting statements.

supporting statements

1
Your body is what's given by nature and by your parents. You should never change it.

2
Cosmetic surgery can give you better chances in life.

3
Women can be beautiful by wearing makeup. Cosmetic surgery is not necessary.

4
Your ideas and values might change in time.

5
Simple cosmetic surgery is getting more common these days. It's not a big deal.

6
You should learn how safe cosmetic surgery is before you have an operation.

Now compare with a classmate.

Work in a group of three. Ask your partners:
Do you agree with Pablo? Do you agree with Ray? Do you agree with Amber?
Answer for each person: *I really agree / I agree / I disagree / I really disagree.*

WHAT ARE YOUR VALUES?

Should people have cosmetic surgery? State your position and support your ideas.
Use new ideas in addition to the ideas above.

Your Position ➤ Supporting Statements ➤

CLARIFYING & EXCHANGING

Now form groups and discuss your position and supporting statements.

ROLE PLAY

Work with a partner. One of you is A, one of you is B. Read your "roles." Have a conversation.

A
You have an attractive girlfriend/boyfriend (B). You are in love. One day, at B's house, you find a photo of her/him from five years ago. B looks totally different. B had cosmetic surgery! You are shocked and say...

useful phrases
Is this really you?   Why?
That's really...   I'm not sure if I...

B
You had cosmetic surgery about five years ago. You have not told A, your boyfriend/girlfriend. A asks you about it.

useful phrases
It's not a big deal.   I feel more...
Now I can...   Before, I...

4

5

VALUES of PEOPLE
I Can't Say No.

SITUATION ∩ **Brad is a busy man, but somehow he is always helping people. Read his story. What is his problem?**

I hate to admit it, but I think I have a problem. Actually, I'm not sure what my problem is. But whatever it is, I need help.

It seems like I'm always doing favors for people, and I never have time for myself. I mean, I like people, and I want them to like me, but it's getting to be too much.

You see, like this week, I'm taking care of Rex. It's a dog that belongs to a woman in my office. How did I end up taking care of this dog? I don't even like dogs. I guess, it was in the office, and Sheila mentioned[1] that she was having trouble finding a dog-sitter[2], and she said if she couldn't find a dog-sitter, she couldn't go on vacation. And suddenly I said, "Oh, I can take care of the dog for you. No problem." Why did I say that? I always seem to get into this kind of situation.

Just last week, this guy across the hall had a problem with his toilet. So he called me! And I don't even know this guy. He said that another neighbor said that I was really good at fixing things, and that she was sure I would be willing[3] to help him, so how could I say no? So I fixed it, and I really didn't mind[4], it only took me about an hour.

It's not only my neighbors and people at work. Like yesterday, my brother needed helping fixing a broken window. I drove two hours to his house to help. It only took ten minutes to repair, but my whole day was shot[5]. And Rex chewed up my sofa while I was gone. These sorts of things happen to me all the time.

Oh, there's the phone. That's probably Emily. She's moving out this weekend, and I told her I'd help her pack. I just couldn't say no.

Oh, what am I going to do?

CHECK YOUR UNDERSTANDING

1. What are some things Brad is doing to help people he knows?
....

2. Why do people ask Brad for help?
....

3. What does Brad want to change about himself?
....

POINTS OF VIEW

Read these three opinions.

Trin

Brad needs to learn to say no. He should refuse to help people. ▢ ▢

Monica

Brad should help only his family and close friends. ▢ ▢

Koji

Brad is lucky that people need him. He should be happy that he can help people. ▢ ▢

Match the supporting statements with the opinions. Write the numbers in the boxes.
Each opinion has two supporting statements.

supporting statements

1
We can't do everything.

2
Brad needs to focus on his own activities.

3
He needs to show his friends that his time is important.

4
Sometimes when we help people we get in trouble.

5
Some people like to have busy lives.

6
Kindness is always returned.

Now compare with a classmate.

Work in a group of three. Ask your partners:
Do you agree with Trin? Do you agree with Monica ? Do you agree with Koji?
Answer for each person: *I really agree / I agree / I disagree / I really disagree.*

WHAT ARE YOUR VALUES?

What advice would you give to Brad? Write your advice and your reasons.
Use new ideas in addition to the ideas above.

Advice	Reasons

CLARIFYING & EXCHANGING

Now form groups and discuss your advice and reasons.

COMMUNICATION ACTIVITY

How do you feel about helping other people? What would you do in these situations?

Lend a friend money	Yes	Yes, but [Limit: $_____]	No
Help a friend move	Yes	Yes, but [Limit: _____hours]	No
Give someone a seat on a crowded train or bus	Yes	Yes, but [Conditions: _____]	No
Let a friend live with me	Yes	Yes, but [Conditions: _____]	No
Share my umbrella with a stranger	Yes	Yes, but [Conditions: _____]	No
Look after my friend's pet	Yes	Yes, but [Conditions: _____]	No
Give a friend a ride home	Yes	Yes, but [Conditions: _____]	No
Help my friend with a home repair	Yes	Yes, but [Conditions: _____]	No
your idea:...	Yes	Yes, but [Conditions: _____]	No

Share your answers with a classmate.

6 Embarrassing Mother!

WARM UP
1. Are your parents fashionable?
2. What famous people are fashionable even though they aren't young?
3. Are age and fashion related?

SITUATION ∩ Risa is 15. Her mother is now 40 years old. Risa thinks her mother is acting strange. Why does Risa think this?

Marie: Risa, I just saw your mom. It's so cool[1] that she dresses that way. She looks so young and hip[2].

Risa: Young? Hip? Ugh! She's so embarrassing[3]! She's driving me crazy[4] with the way that she's always trying to wear young clothes and talk to you guys about music and stuff.

Marie: But I don't mind at all. I really like your mom. She's fun.

Risa: It's not fun for me. It's been crazy ever since her 40th birthday. She's been trying to act like she's our age or something. It's just wrong. She wants to go shopping at the same stores as me, and half the time I can't even find my fashion magazines because she "borrows" them.

Marie: Really?

Risa: She bleached[5] her hair, she started wearing these little tops and short skirts. And now she says she might get a tattoo[6]!

Marie: No way!

Risa: If she does that I seriously won't go out in public with her anymore.

Marie: I think it's kind of cool that she wants to be your friend. She's a lot better than my mom. With her it's always "Where are you going? When are you coming back? Who are you going with?" I mean, I would love it if she took me shopping or asked me for fashion advice.

Risa: Yeah, but my mom has gone completely overboard[7]. And my dad, too. I mean, he isn't any help. He says she looks prettier and sexier than ever. "You are just like a good wine," he says, "more delicious with age." Eeewwww!

Marie: Eeewwww!

Risa: It's disgusting!

CHECK YOUR UNDERSTANDING

1. What is Risa's mother's new fashion style?
....
2. Why doesn't Risa like it?
....
3. What does Marie think?
....

. Read these three opinions.

James

Risa's mother is having problems, and Risa should try to
help her.

Amber

Risa does not have to like what
her mother is doing, but she
should accept it.

Ray

Risa should encourage her
mother, and be happy that she is
having such fun.

Match the supporting statements with the opinions. Write the numbers in the boxes.
Each opinion has two supporting statements.

supporting statements

1

Sharing fashion styles is a great
opportunity to enjoy doing things
together.

2

Perhaps her mother has a lot of
stress in her life. She needs support.

3

Children should respect their parents.

4

Risa should take her mother to
see a doctor.

5

Risa should not worry about what
her friends think of her mother.

6

Risa should be happy that her
mother is enjoying life.

Now compare with a classmate.

Work in a group of three. Ask your partners:
Do you agree with James? Do you agree with Amber? Do you agree with Ray?
Answer for each person: *I really agree / I agree / I disagree / I really disagree.*

WHAT ARE YOUR VALUES?

What would you do in Risa's situation? State your position and support your ideas.
Use new ideas in addition to the ideas above.

Your Position

Supporting Statements

CLARIFYING & EXCHANGING

Now form groups and
discuss your position and
supporting statements.

COMMUNICATION ACTIVITY

Give a presentation about "Me when I'm 40." Talk about:

- Personality
- Lifestyle
- Romance
- Free time activities
- Fashion
- Responsibilities

example
When I am 40 I will be (the same... more careful...).
I will (live in... be married... work for...).
For fun, I will (go out with friends... play golf... take my family to...).

V A L U E S in RELATIONSHIPS

In this section, you can discuss different ideas about
what is important in a relationship.

Newlyweds

Is it important for men to know
how to do certain things around
the house?

Is it important for women to know
how to do certain things around
the house?

A newlywed couple finds out that
marriage isn't exactly what they
expected.

8 Stanley in Love

How should you let someone know
you're attracted to them?

Is it okay to go to extremes for love?

A man explains that his friend might
have an unusual idea about love

9 Always Late!

What can we do to show respect to
someone?

What kinds of things show disrespect?

A woman has trouble being on time.
Her fiance talks about it with his father.

The Computer Nut

Is technology a positive or negative influence on your life?

How does technology affect your relationships?

A man loves using his computer, but his wife is worried about it.

A Secret Romance

How do you decide to trust someone?

Is it okay to keep a romance secret?

A young single woman talks about her relationship with an older married man.

Staying Together

Should couples stay together even if they have serious problems?

What might cause you to break up with a boyfriend or girlfriend?

A woman is very worried about her boyfriend's behavior when he's angry.

VALUES in RELATIONSHIPS
Newlyweds

WARM UP
1. What household chores are necessary to do? Make a list.
2. Which do you like to do? Which do you avoid?

SITUATION 🎧 Sam and Cheryl are newlyweds. They're talking to their friends about their marriage. How is their marriage going?

Keith: Hey, Sam, congratulations! I haven't seen you since you got married. How are things going?

Sam: Ah, it's not like I thought it'd be.

Keith: Really? I thought you were in love with Cheryl. She seems like a wonderful person.

Sam: Yes, she is, but...

Keith: But what?

Sam: She can't cook. Please don't laugh at me. I'm serious. She cannot cook.

Keith: So what? Lots of people can't cook.

Sam: No, you don't understand. I mean, she really can't cook. I mean, she tries, but she can't even cook rice or make toast without burning it, and she tries to make these special dishes, but they're just inedible[1]. They're nothing at all like my mother used to make for me.

Keith: Well, maybe it's just that you have to get used to her style. And maybe you should learn to cook. Ever thought of that?

Sam: Me? Cook? Come on. That's a woman's job.

Heidi: Hey, hi, Cheryl. I haven't seen you since you got married. Congratulations.

Cheryl: Thanks.

Heidi: How are things going?

Cheryl: Ah, well, not as... not as well as I thought.

Heidi: What do you mean? I... I thought you were in love with Sam.

Cheryl: Well, I am.

Heidi: Well, he seems like a great guy.

Cheryl: Oh, oh, he is. He is, but...

Heidi: But what?

Cheryl: Well, I don't know. Well, he... he's such a... well, he's a klutz[2].

Heidi: A klutz? What do you mean?

Cheryl: Well, you know we bought an old house, and it needs a lot of work, and, well, I just assumed that Sam knew how to fix things.

Heidi: You did?

Cheryl: But, you know, he can't even change a light bulb! Oh, it's such a disaster[3]. You know, I remember my father and my brothers — they all knew how to fix things, and build things, and... Why can't Sam?

Heidi: Well, I don't know. Well, maybe, Cheryl, that not all guys are good at that kind of stuff. And, you know, have you ever thought about learning how to fix things yourself?

Cheryl: Me?

Heidi: Yeah.

Cheryl: Fix things? Come on. That's a man's job.

CHECK YOUR UNDERSTANDING

1. What is Sam worried about?

....

2. What is Cheryl worried about?

....

3. What do their friends think?

....

Read these three opinions.

Koji

Cheryl should learn to cook and Sam should learn to fix things. ▢ ▢

Carmen

They should get divorced. ▢ ▢

Pablo

Sam and Cheryl should just accept each other the way they are. ▢ ▢

Match the supporting statements with the opinions. Write the numbers in the boxes.
Each opinion has two supporting statements.

supporting statements

1

Sam simply needs to learn how to fix things. He didn't learn from his father.

2

It's important for people to understand each other's strengths and weaknesses.

3

They don't really love one another. If they did, they would not complain about each other.

4

These are minor problems in a relationship. Sam and Cheryl shouldn't worry about them.

5

Cheryl simply needs to learn how to cook. She didn't learn from her mother.

6

They will never appreciate each other, because they keep comparing their spouse to their parents.

Now compare with a classmate.

Work in a group of three. Ask your partners:
Do you agree with Koji? Do you agree with Carmen? Do you agree with Pablo?
Answer for each person: *I really agree / I agree / I disagree / I really disagree.*

WHAT ARE YOUR VALUES?

What do you think about gender roles in a relationship? State your position and support your ideas.
Use new ideas in addition to the ideas above.

Your Position ▶ Supporting Statements ▶

> **CLARIFYING & EXCHANGING**
>
> Now form groups and discuss your position and supporting statements.

DISCUSSION ACTIVITY

Make a list of things that: men generally do but women don't often do; women generally do but men don't often do; both men and women do. Think about:

work
clothes/appearance
home activities
sports
language

Work in a group of four. Compare your lists. Is there a good reason for any of these?

8 Stanley in Love

WARM UP
1. Are you shy?
2. Would you ask someone on a date even if they might say "no"?
3. Do you change when you fall in love?

SITUATION

Stanley is in love — or is he? Is this really love? Mark, his best friend, is worried about Stanley. Why is Mark worried?

I've got a problem. My best friend, Stanley, has never dated anyone, and he's kind of shy and sensitive[1], and now he says he's madly in love[2] with a woman. Her name is Lian, and she recently started working at the department store where Stanley and I work part-time.

As soon as Stanley saw Lian, he thought she was the most beautiful woman he'd ever seen! That's okay, I mean, she is really attractive, but I think he's going too far. He told me that Lian secretly likes him, but that she's too shy to admit it. That's a little weird[3], because she's not shy at all.

Lian is really cute, but I think she might have a boyfriend, and, to be honest, I don't think Stanley is her type[4].

The other day, Stanley told me "I've got to find out more about her." And I thought, oh, you're going to ask her out? But no, he didn't ask her out. He secretly followed her home from work to find out where she lives! I thought, oh, no, this is weird, and I told him he shouldn't do that — that he could get in trouble. He told me I was overreacting[5], that he was just curious about her.

Now, though, I'm getting really worried. Stanley was talking about Lian, and said that he was thinking about calling her. I thought, good, he's finally being direct[6]. And he said that it was better to call her at home than trying to talk to her at work. When I asked if she gave him her number, he said no, that he looked at the employee files[7]. We're really not supposed to do that.

I don't know what I should do. I tried to talk to him about it, but he just got mad and stopped talking to me. I don't know if he has called Lian, or whether she even knows that he likes her. I think he might be turning into a stalker[8].

CHECK YOUR UNDERSTANDING

1. How is Stanley acting toward Lian? ....
2. What is Lian like? ....
3. Does Lian know how Stanley feels? ....
4. What is Mark going to do? ....

Read these three opinions.

Amber

Mark should insist that Stanley stop, even if it ends his friendship with Stanley. ▢ ▢

Trin

Mark shouldn't say anything to Stanley, but he should warn Lian. ▢ ▢

Ray

Mark should wait and see what happens before doing anything. ▢ ▢

**Match the supporting statements with the opinions. Write the numbers in the boxes.
Each opinion has two supporting statements.**

supporting statements

1

It's probably not serious, but it's better if she knows.

2

It's important not to accuse someone until you are sure.

3

You have to stop problems before they get out of control.

4

Stanley will probably stop once he realizes she's not interested in him.

5

He has to do something, but it could be dangerous to upset Stanley.

6

Sometimes we need a friend to tell us the ugly truth.

Now compare with a classmate.

Work in a group of three. Ask your partners:
Do you agree with Amber? Do you agree with Trin? Do you agree with Ray?
Answer for each person: *I really agree / I agree / I disagree / I really disagree.*

WHAT ARE YOUR VALUES?

What advice would you give to Mark? Write your advice and your reasons.
Use new ideas in addition to the ideas above.

Advice	Reasons

CLARIFYING & EXCHANGING

Now form groups and discuss your advice and reasons.

DISCUSSION ACTIVITY

What's the best way to meet someone for a date?

.... part-time job
.... school
.... work
.... family introduction
.... through a friend
.... Internet

.... personal ad in the newspaper
.... bars and social clubs
.... hobby groups
.... on vacation
your idea: ....

Compare your answers with a partner. Do you know someone who met and fell in love in any of these ways?

9

V A L U E S in **RELATIONSHIPS**

Always Late!

WARM UP
1. Are you usually on time for school? For meetings?
2. What is a good reason for being late?

SITUATION 🎧 **Duksoo is a Korean American. He's talking with his father about his fiancee. But his father thinks there is a problem. What is the problem?**

Father: We've been waiting almost half an hour now. Where's Jinhee?

Duksoo: I don't know. I guess she's late again.

Father: You mean this has happened before?

Duksoo: Yeah. All the time.

Father: Really? And this is the woman you're engaged to, and planning to marry?

Duksoo: Yes, of course! She's beautiful, she's kind, she's really a wonderful person, Dad. And I know she'll be a great mother. So what if she runs late[1] sometimes? It's really not that big a deal[2].

Father: Okay, but being late is a sign of disrespect[3]. It shows a lack of respect for other people, for commitments. It's a sign of a bigger problem.

Duksoo: No, it's nothing like that. Believe me. She's not disrespectful, she's just, um... disorganized[4].

Father: Disorganized? Well, let me make sure I understand. She's really this late all the time?

Duksoo: Yes. To tell the truth, sometimes it's even worse. Like yesterday, we had an appointment at 5 o'clock to talk with the manager of the Prince Hotel.

Father: Where the wedding is going to be? That's a very important meeting.

Duksoo: I know. So I arrived on time, at 5. But Jinhee didn't come until almost 6. Actually, it was really embarrassing[5]. But, Dad, she didn't mean it. She said that...

Father: An hour late. I had no idea it was that bad. That is rude[6]. That's very selfish. Very disrespectful. Have you talked to her about it?

Duksoo: Of course I have. Over and over. But if I bring it up too often she gets angry, and tells me to relax.

Father: You're trying to help her with her problem, and she gets angry at you. That's even more disrespectful. It's obvious that the problem is deeper than just being late. If you marry her, you're going to have a lot of trouble.

Duksoo: Ahh...

CHECK YOUR UNDERSTANDING

1. Why is Jinhee late a lot? ....
2. Does it bother Duksoo? ....
3. What does Duksoo's father think? ....
4. What does Jinhee think? ....

POINTS OF VIEW

Read these three opinions.

Pablo

People cannot be changed.

James

People who are late are rude and lazy.

Carmen

Everyone is different.

Match the supporting statements with the opinions. Write the numbers in the boxes.
Each opinion has two supporting statements.

supporting statements

1

We should enjoy people who see the world differently.

2

Some people are late by nature.

3

Live and let live! The world would be dull if everybody were the same.

4

Some parts of a person's character are genetic.

5

There is no excuse for being late.

6

People can be on time if they try.

Now compare with a classmate.

Work in a group of three. Ask your partners:
Do you agree with Pablo? Do you agree with James? Do you agree with Carmen?
Answer for each person: *I really agree / I agree / I disagree / I really disagree.*

WHAT ARE YOUR VALUES?

What should Duksoo do? Write your advice and your reasons.
Use new ideas in addition to the ideas above.

Advice

Reasons

CLARIFYING & EXCHANGING

Now form groups and discuss your advice and reasons.

PERSONAL STORY

What is the latest you have been for something (a meeting, a class, an interview, an airplane...)? Why were you late? What happened? Think about the situation, and write some notes.

notes:
took place in: ....   main event: ....
your reaction: ....   other people's reaction: ....
what you learned: ....

Tell your story to the class.

9

VALUES in RELATIONSHIPS

The Computer Nut

WARM UP

1. How long do you use a computer every day?

2. What do you use a computer for? School? Work? Entertainment?

3. Do you know someone who uses a computer a lot? What does he or she do on the computer?

4. What is "too much" computer use?

SITUATION ∩ Read the conversation between Susan and Ken and find out why their marriage is in trouble.

Susan: Sweetie[1], do you know what day it is?

Ken: Excuse me, but I'm very busy right now. I have to answer this email.

Susan: You forgot, didn't you?

Ken: What? Did you say something? Can't you wait until tomorrow? I'm real busy[2] right now.

Susan: Agh![3]

Ken: Why are you sitting on my keyboard? Look what you've done!

Susan: You forgot my birthday!

Ken: Is it today? Really? Today? Let me check my appointment[4] file on my computer. Please get off my keyboard.

Susan: You don't have to check your computer file. My birthday is TODAY! This is your wife talking to you. Do you need to check your computer file to see who I am?

Ken: Okay, okay. I believe you. I'm sorry. I'm... I'm really, really sorry. Now, please get off my keyboard and... and I'll send you an email birthday card.

Susan: Agh! What is wrong with you?[5] You spend all of your time with your computer. Do you still love me?

Ken: Of course I do. Now, if you get off my keyboard, I'll order some flowers from the flower shop's website.

Susan: I don't care about flowers. I'm worried about us and about you. Do you remember when we were first married? We used to do so many things together. We used to hike in the mountains, we used to ride our bikes...

Ken: You know I remember. But that was before computers. Now I use my computer to go anywhere in the world. I can hike mountains in Europe and go bike riding in China.

Susan: But that's not real. And I'm not with you. I'm worried about your health. You spend all day with your computer at your office and then all night and the weekends with your computer at home. It's not healthy.

Ken: But I'm happy. I love my computers, okay? But, because I love you, I will see my doctor and get a checkup[6], all right? Now, please get off my keyboard and I'll send an email to my doctor to make an appointment.

CHECK YOUR UNDERSTANDING

1. How does Susan feel? Why? ....

2. How does Ken feel? Why? ....

3. How has the computer changed their life?.................................

POINTS OF VIEW

Read these three opinions.

Trin

Ken should spend less time with his computer and more time with his wife.

James

Computers destroy human relationships.

Monica

Susan should share her husband's interest in the computer.

Match the supporting statements with the opinions. Write the numbers in the boxes.
Each opinion has two supporting statements.

supporting statements

1

Susan should understand how important computers are to Ken.

2

Husbands and wives should share each other's interests and hobbies.

3

A spouse is more important than a machine.

4

We need to have a balance in our lives.

5

Computers are convenient but harmful.

6

It is not healthy to spend a lot of time with a computer.

Now compare with a classmate.

Work in a group of three. Ask your partners:
Do you agree with Trin? Do you agree with James? Do you agree with Monica?
Answer for each person: *I really agree / I agree / I disagree / I really disagree.*

WHAT ARE YOUR VALUES?

What advice would you give to Ken and Susan? Write your advice and your reasons.
Use new ideas in addition to the ideas above.

Advice	Reasons

CLARIFYING & EXCHANGING

Now form groups and discuss your advice and reasons.

DISCUSSION ACTIVITY

How does technology affect your life?
Work with a partner. Talk about each object. Do you use it? Do you like it? Why or why not?

digital map system

iPod

computer

cell phone

digital music player

your idea: _____

10

VALUES in RELATIONSHIPS
A Secret Romance

WARM UP

1. What is your opinion of married people having relationships outside of their marriage?

2. Is it okay to have secrets from your spouse? About what?

3. Is divorce okay in some cases?

SITUATION 🎧 **Diane is having a relationship with a married man. She's writing in her diary about this relationship. What do you think will happen between her and Frank?**

Dear Diary,

Today is our first anniversary[1]! Frank and I have been together for one year. We had a lovely lunch at DeNiro's, our favorite restaurant. Of course, I was disappointed that we couldn't have dinner together, since he has to be with his wife and his children. I understand that. But next week, he's going on a business trip for two days, and I'm going with him. I can't wait!

I can't help saying it again: I love Frank deeply, with all of my heart. I know I've written this before. I can't help it! He is so different from other men. He is handsome and intelligent. But, more importantly, he talks to me and listens to me.

The problem is his wife, Louise. Louise learned the truth last week. She insists she doesn't want a divorce. Frank told her he doesn't love her anymore, and that he's truly in love with me. But she still wants him! I understand. I would not want to let go of[2] Frank. But she's being unrealistic[3]. She's going to lose him.

Frank told me that he wants a divorce but the time is not right yet. He still has to figure out[4] what will happen with his two teenage children after the divorce. I haven't told anyone about Frank. Except I did tell my best friend, Virginia. She thinks I'm crazy and says that Frank's a liar[5]. She said that he's cheated on[6] his wife—that he's been unfaithful[7] to her and that you can't trust a man like Frank. And Virginia also told me that most married men stay with their wives.

But I don't believe Virginia. I know that I love Frank, and that he and I will get married and will start our own family together. For now, I just have to trust that everything will be all right.

CHECK YOUR UNDERSTANDING

1. Does Frank's wife know about his relationship with Diane?

....

2. How does Diane feel about Frank's wife and family?

....

3. What does Diane's friend Virginia think?

....

Read these three opinions.

Carmen

Diane loves Frank very much and will be a good wife.

Ray

Frank should stop seeing Diane until he gets a divorce.

Trin

When a couple has children, divorce is wrong.

Match the supporting statements with the opinions. Write the numbers in the boxes.
Each opinion has two supporting statements.

supporting statements

1

Children are always hurt when their parents are divorced.

2

Love is the foundation of a strong marriage.

3

It is wrong for a married person to have a lover.

4

When two people love one another, they will have a good marriage.

5

Children need to be with their mother and father.

6

Honesty and respect is important in any relationship.

Now compare with a classmate.

Work in a group of three. Ask your partners:
Do you agree with Carmen? Do you agree with Ray? Do you agree with Trin?
Answer for each person: *I really agree / I agree / I disagree / I really disagree.*

WHAT ARE YOUR VALUES?

Are relationships like this okay? State your position and support your ideas.
Use new ideas in addition to the ideas above.

Your Position

Supporting Statements

CLARIFYING & EXCHANGING

Now form groups and discuss your position and supporting statements.

VALUES EXCHANGE

You are Louise's best friend. She asks you for advice. What advice will you give Louise?
Circle one or write your own.

A. Louise should allow Frank to have a relationship with Diane.
B. Louise should divorce Frank, even if he stops seeing Diane.
C. Louise should stay with Frank, but only if he stops seeing Diane.

your idea: ....

Write a letter to Louise. Give your advice. Exchange letters with a partner. Do you agree with your partner?

VALUES in RELATIONSHIPS

Staying Together

1. Have you ever been really, really angry? When? What was the reason? What did you do?

2. Has anyone ever become really angry at you? When? What was the reason? What did you do?

SITUATION ∩ **Annie needs advice about her relationship with her boyfriend. She's talking to her best friend, Tess, about it.**

What's Annie's problem?

Tess: Annie, you look upset[1]. Is... is something wrong?

Annie: Yeah, it's Dan.

Tess: Dan? What... what's wrong?

Annie: Well, a couple of days ago, he called me from work and he said he'd be home at 7:00. So, I had dinner ready, but, 7:00 — he didn't come home. About an hour later, I called his office, and nobody answered.

Tess: Strange.

Annie: I left a message for him to call me. And then at 9:00 I called his cell phone, but it was turned off.

Tess: It seems like if he had to work, he should have called.

Annie: Yeah. So, after midnight he finally came home, and he was really drunk.

Tess: Oh, wow. Yeah, you know, he drinks too much.

Annie: I know. Well, I told him that he should have at least called me.

Tess: Yeah. Of course.

Annie: But he told me that I was being bossy[2].

Tess: Really!

Annie: He yelled[3] at me and he told me to shut up!

Tess: Well, that's terrible!

Annie: Yeah. I was really mad, and I told him that I wasn't his slave[4].

Tess: Well, good for you!

Annie: I don't know. After that, he got really angry. He started yelling at me, and he grabbed[5] my arm.

Tess: No.

Annie: And he pushed me against the refrigerator.

Tess: Really?

Annie: Yeah. So I screamed, and he hit me.

Tess: What? He hit you? Oh, I... I can't believe it. That... that's terrible!

Annie: I know. I decided right then that I was going to break up with[6] him. I was so shocked[7] and so scared.

Tess: Yeah.

Annie: But the next day, well, he came home from work and he brought me flowers. He said that he was really sorry for what happened. He told me that he needs me. He also told me that his boss is causing a lot of trouble for him at work, and that he's really stressed. And he promised[8] that he would stop drinking.

Tess: Do you believe him? Do you think he really will? What are you going to do?

Annie: I don't know. I really want to believe him. It's hard to imagine him changing. I don't know what to do.

CHECK YOUR UNDERSTANDING

1. What made Dan angry?..
2. What did he do? ....
3. How did Tess react? ....

Read these three opinions.

Trin

Annie should break up immediately with Dan.

Koji

Annie should give Dan another chance, and not talk about it.

Monica

Annie should tell Dan how she feels, and try to discuss the problem.

Match the supporting statements with the opinions. Write the numbers in the boxes.
Each opinion has two supporting statements.

supporting statements

1

He is obviously sorry, and she shouldn't overreact.

2

Dan seems to be under stress, and Annie should try to help.

3

Everyone gets angry once in a while.

4

Dan has serious problems. Things will get worse.

5

He'll soon forget his promises. Annie can't trust him.

6

Communication is the key to solving this kind of problem.

Now compare with a classmate.

Work in a group of three. Ask your partners:
Do you agree with Trin? Do you agree with Koji? Do you agree with Monica?
Answer for each person: *I really agree / I agree / I disagree / I really disagree.*

WHAT ARE YOUR VALUES?

What advice would you give to Annie? Give your advice and your reasons.
Use new ideas in addition to the ideas above.

Advice	Reasons

CLARIFYING & EXCHANGING

Now form groups and discuss your advice and reasons.

ROLE PLAY

Read the advice that counselors might give. Check the ones you agree with. Then have a role play.

.... Show all your feelings. It's okay to argue!
.... Talk about your problems calmly and rationally.
.... Don't discuss important things when you are upset.
.... Schedule time to talk about your relationship.
.... Being a good listener is the most important skill.
my idea: ....

A
You are a relationship counselor. Ask many questions about Student B's relationship. Give advice on how to improve things.
example
How is your relationship with...?
How did you feel about...?
You could...

B
You are having trouble with your relationship. You ask a relationship counselor (Student A) for help. Explain the things your partner does that you don't like. Ask for advice.
example
My boyfriend/girlfriend always...
What should I do?

VALUES in the WORKPLACE

In this section, you'll find out about different workplace attitudes and beliefs.

13 Shen's Boss

What should you do if a co-worker treats you unfairly?

What should you do if a boss treats you unfairly?

Shen thinks his boss is treating him unfairly, and he doesn't know what to do.

14 Naomi's Dilemma

Is it okay to date someone you work with?

Are "office romances" common in your cult

Naomi's boss asked her on a date. She tells brother how she feels about it.

15 Drinking Workers

Do some jobs have "unwritten rules"?

If a worker doesn't agree with the company rules, what should she or he do?

An employee explains why he doesn't want to go out after work with his boss and co-workers.

16 Dress for Success

How do we talk about problems we have at work?

Should teachers be able to dress any way they want?

A teacher explains why she is concerned about another teacher's appearance.

17 A Chocolate Lover's Nightmare

Is it okay to hide a mistake?

What should you do if your istake hurts other people?

A woman talks about making an embarrassing mistake at work.

18 Career Choice

What is important to you in a job?

What do you need to be happy in life?

A young graduate has to choose between two different companies.

13 Shen's Boss

SITUATION 🎧 **Shen has a problem in his office. He emails his American friend, John, for advice. As you read their emails, think about this: Do they agree on what Shen should do?**

Shen:

Hi, John, how's everything going? Did you have a good weekend? Do you remember that I wrote you about the new boss in my office? I was excited because he seemed to be a great guy, very polite and easy to get along with. Well, unfortunately, I was wrong. He's not so easy to get along with. At least not for me. I don't think he likes me. When we're alone, he's mean[1] to me. He speaks harshly[2], and criticizes[3] my work. And he doesn't joke with me or act friendly, like he does with other employees[4]. But when other people are around, he's very polite to me. The rest of the workers in the office say he is terrific[5]! Everyone likes him. I will try to do my best, and hope the new boss changes his mind. What do you think I should do?

John:

Shen, thanks for your email. Yes, I had a great weekend. But I am sorry to hear about your new boss. It sounds like you need to do something! Do you have any idea why he doesn't like you? Did you do something to make him angry?

Shen:

I don't think I did anything wrong. I think he just doesn't like me. Yesterday he gave me a list of 500 people to contact and told me that I had to reach[6] everyone by Monday—in three days. It's going to be impossible! Three people couldn't do it in a week! I'll do my best, but I'm worried that he's setting me up to fail[7]. I really think he just wants to fire[8] me and this is his way of doing it.

John:

Shen, you've got to do something! Don't let him get away with it.[9] Your new boss is trying to fire you. You need to talk to him directly. Tell him that you feel you're being mistreated[10]. Ask him if he thinks he's being fair to you! Or maybe you should talk to the president of the company. Good luck!

Shen:

Thanks, John, for your advice. But there's no way I can do what you suggest. It's impossible for me to ask my boss what is wrong. We can't do that here. And going to the president, well, that would even be more difficult. In this country, you don't go over your boss's head[11] and talk to the president. I will continue to try[12] to do my best. If he fires me, I'll have to accept that.

Read these three opinions.

Monica

Shen should talk directly to his boss. ▭ ▭

Pablo

Shen should find a new job. ▭ ▭

Koji

Shen should say nothing, and continue to do his best. ▭ ▭

Match the supporting statements with the opinions. Write the numbers in the boxes.
Each opinion has two supporting statements.

supporting statements

1
Sometimes it is a good idea to find out what is going on.

2
Complaining often leads to more difficulties.

3
It is easier to find a new job when you already have a job.

4
When your boss doesn't like you, then you should quit.

5
Show everyone your value by working hard and not causing trouble.

6
Direct action is usually a good way to correct a problem or misunderstanding.

Now compare with a classmate.

Work in a group of three. Ask your partners:
Do you agree with Monica? Do you agree with Pablo? Do you agree with Koji?
Answer for each person: *I really agree / I agree / I disagree / I really disagree.*

WHAT ARE YOUR VALUES?

What advice would you give to Shen? Why? Give your advice and your reasons.
Use new ideas in addition to the ideas above.

Advice ▶ Reasons ▶

CLARIFYING & EXCHANGING

Now form groups and discuss your advice and reasons.

VALUES ACTIVITY

What makes a good employee? Someone who...

	Yes	No		Yes	No
works hard all of the time	....	....	has a life outside of the office	....	....
comes to work on time	....	....	is respectful to the boss	....	....
leaves work at the end of the day	....	....	is respectful to fellow workers	....	....
always stays late	....	....	doesn't complain	....	....
never takes a vacation	....	....	your idea:		
takes a vacation	....	....			

Exchange your ideas with a classmate.

14 Naomi's Dilemma

WARM UP

1. Are you more comfortable with a man or a woman teacher? Does it matter?

2. Are you more comfortable with a man or a woman boss? Does it matter?

SITUATION

🎧 **Naomi calls her brother, Tom, to ask for advice about a situation at work. What is the problem? What is she afraid of?**

Tom:	Hello.
Naomi:	Hey, Tom. It's me.
Tom:	Oh, hey, Naomi. What's wrong?
Naomi:	I need your advice. I... I have a problem at work.
Tom:	Let's hear it.
Naomi:	Well, it's... it's my boss.
Tom:	What did he do?
Naomi:	He's... he's acting weird[1].
Tom:	I thought you liked him.
Naomi:	I did, up until yesterday.
Tom:	What happened?
Naomi:	Well... okay. I had just sent him this long email updating[2] him on a really cool project I was working on, and he called me into his office and I thought he was going to talk about that. But then he asked me out[3].
Tom:	On a date?
Naomi:	Yeah. It was really uncomfortable.
Tom:	Oh, I get it[4]. So, you don't like him that way[5].
Naomi:	I thought he was great, until he did that, you know? Now I don't know what to think. It was just so inappropriate[6]. It was creepy[7].
Tom:	Creepy? I mean, is he older than you?
Naomi:	No, not really. A few years, maybe.
Tom:	Well, I mean, is he married?
Naomi:	No.
Tom:	Did he act weird with you?
Naomi:	No, not... act weird with me.
Tom:	Did he threaten[8] to fire you if you didn't go out with him or something?
Naomi:	No, he was actually very polite. But, wait. That's not the point. He shouldn't ask me for a date at work like that. It's not right. It's going to mess everything up[9].
Tom:	Naomi, dating nowadays, it's becoming a lot more common in the workplace.
Naomi:	Tom, don't you get it? He's my boss! I'm afraid he might fire me if I say no.
Tom:	I don't think it'll come to that[10]. Listen. Things are really changing nowadays. I'm not sure those old rules apply anymore. And, I mean, you're both adults, and you like each other, so why not give it a shot[11]?
Naomi:	I don't know if that's such a good idea. But thanks for your advice anyway.
Tom:	Yeah. What are big brothers for?

CHECK YOUR UNDERSTANDING

1. Naomi became uncomfortable. What did Naomi's boss do?

....

2. What does Naomi think about dating in offices?

....

3. What is Tom's advice?

....

POINTS OF VIEW

Read these three opinions.

Carmen

Naomi should go out with her boss one time. ▢ ▢

Anton

Naomi should find a new job first, and then quit her job. ▢ ▢

Trin

Naomi should complain to some-one in the company. ▢ ▢

Match the supporting statements with the opinions. Write the numbers in the boxes.
Each opinion has two supporting statements.

supporting statements

1

In life, we often have to do things that we don't want to do.

2

Sometimes people worry too much.

3

When we think we are right, we must not give up.

4

People who do wrong things have to be exposed.

5

It is hopeless to complain.

6

If a situation is hopeless, then we need to be clever and find a solution.

Now compare with a classmate.

Work in a group of three. Ask your partners:
Do you agree with Carmen? Do you agree with Anton? Do you agree with Trin?
Answer for each person: *I really agree / I agree / I disagree / I really disagree.*

WHAT ARE YOUR VALUES?

What advice would you give to Naomi? Write your advice and your reasons.
Use new ideas in addition to the ideas above.

Advice	Reasons

CLARIFYING & EXCHANGING

Now form groups and discuss your advice and reasons.

VALUES EXCHANGE

What makes a good boss? Someone who is...

	Yes	No		Yes	No
a man	....	....	well-educated	....	....
a woman	....	....	experienced	....	....
older than me	....	....	very formal	....	....
younger than me	....	....	easy to socialize with	....	....
very smart	....	....	your ideas:		

Exchange your ideas with a classmate.

14

WARM UP
1. Should you socialize with your co-workers or your boss? Why or why not?

2. Should you keep your personal life separate from your work? Why or why not?

SITUATION ∩ **Mark, a Canadian software engineer, has been working in Tokyo for six months. His company, Intensa Corp., is international, but most of the Tokyo staff is Japanese, including Mark's boss, Mr. Tanaka. He's talking to his fellow worker, Yosuke. As you read their conversation, think about this: How does Mark feel about drinking with the other people who work in the same office?**

Mark: Hi, Yosuke, how's everything?

Yosuke: Hello, Mark. What's happening?

Mark: Oh, not much.

Yosuke: Are you okay these days? I'm a little worried about you.

Mark: Why?

Yosuke: Well, you know, we all went drinking last night, and you didn't join us, and I was wondering...

Mark: Oh, that again.

Yosuke: Yes. We missed you.

Mark: Hmm. Did Mr. Tanaka say anything about my not joining you?

Yosuke: Well, he did say he was worried about how you were getting along with[1] everyone.

Mark: I was afraid of that. I think what he really means is "Why won't Mark go drinking with us?"

Yosuke: Well, Mark, it is important. It's part of the way we do things here in Japan. And actually, we hired[2] you because you speak Japanese and you understand how we do things here.

Mark: I thought you hired me because I was a good engineer, not because I'm a good drinker.

Yosuke: Well, you know what I mean. It's more than that. Often we spend time talking about work things... nothing official[3], but it helps when we're all back at the office. It's part of getting ahead.

Mark: Look, Yosuke, I understand, but I don't want to be pressured[4]. I have to have a personal life. I don't want to spend my free time that way.

Yosuke: But, Mark, that's the only way to get ahead[5] here. Human relations are important if you want to succeed.

Mark: I don't believe that. I'll succeed with my ability, not by getting drunk[6] with my boss. It's unprofessional[7].

Yosuke: But, it's fun. We always have a great time, and we all know each other really well now.

Mark: I know you guys have fun, but... It just seems unprofessional to me.

Yosuke: Okay, well, I respect your opinion[8]. But I don't think that's the way Mr. Tanaka sees it.

CHECK YOUR UNDERSTANDING

1. Why doesn't Mark want to go drinking after work? ....

2. Why does Yosuke think it's important? ....

3. What do you think Mr. Tanaka is going to do about Mark?...

Read these three opinions.

Monica

Mark shouldn't go out drinking. His company shouldn't expect him to.

Koji

Mark should go out drinking. It's part of the culture.

Ray

Mark is right. He'll get ahead by being a good engineer.

Match the supporting statements with the opinions. Write the numbers in the boxes.
Each opinion has two supporting statements.

supporting statements

1

He's not trying hard enough to understand Japanese culture.

2

An international company should adapt to its workers.

3

He shouldn't insist on his cultural values.

4

It's important to focus on your priorities.

5

Drinking has nothing to do with engineering.

6

It's okay if not everyone does the same thing.

Now compare with a classmate.

Work in a group of three. Ask your partners:
Do you agree with Monica? Do you agree with Koji? Do you agree with Ray?
Answer for each person: *I really agree / I agree / I disagree / I really disagree.*

WHAT ARE YOUR VALUES?

What advice would you give to Mark? Give your advice and your reasons.
Use new ideas in addition to the ideas above.

Advice

Reasons

CLARIFYING & EXCHANGING

Now form groups and discuss your advice and reasons.

CULTURE SURVEY

Here are some cultural practices. If you were living in a different culture, which ones would you adapt to?
Write a number (1=easy to adapt, 2=somewhat easy, 3=somewhat hard, 4=very hard to adapt).

.... singing karaoke (Japan)
.... eating dinner at 10 p.m. (Argentina)
.... taking a siesta in the afternoon (Spain)
.... wearing tiny bathing suits (Brazil)
.... giving gifts for many social occasions (China)

.... eating fast food (U.S.)
.... kissing someone to say hello (France)
.... hugging someone to say goodbye (Canada)
your idea:...

Compare with a partner.

16 | VALUES in the WORKPLACE
Dress for Success

1. Is there a formal "dress code" at your office or school? What is it?

2. What do you wear every day? How do you decide?

SITUATION 🎧 **Mia Rios, an English teacher, is talking to the director of her school, Mr. Lee, about another English teacher in the school. What is Ms. Rios complaining about? What does Mr. Lee decide to do?**

Ms. Rios:	Thank you for taking time to see me this morning, Mr. Lee. I know you're very busy.
Mr. Lee:	No problem, Mia. Now, what's on your mind?
Ms. Rios:	Well, it's kind of a touchy subject¹. It's about Ms. Bailey.
Mr. Lee:	Really? Is it something about her teaching? She's one of our best teachers. She always gets high evaluations².
Ms. Rios:	Oh, yes, yes.
Mr. Lee:	The students love her.
Ms. Rios:	Yes, I know that.
Mr. Lee:	Did the two of you have an argument³?
Ms. Rios:	No, no no no. It's... it's nothing like that. It's... well, it's the way she dresses. You know, her short skirts, and her little tops.
Mr. Lee:	Ah, yes. That.
Ms. Rios:	Yes. Yes, the way she dresses. I know it distracts⁴ the students, especially the boys. I mean, just this morning I heard some of them talking in the hall about it.
Mr. Lee:	Well, in fact I did try to bring it up indirectly⁵, but she didn't seem to understand.
Ms. Rios:	Well, could you talk to her again? Don't you — don't we have a responsibility⁶ to the students?
Mr. Lee:	Well, perhaps you can talk to her. You're a woman, and she might...
Ms. Rios:	I can't do that! That's not my place, Mr. Lee. You're the director. It's your responsibility.
Mr. Lee:	I'm not sure I can either.
Ms. Rios:	Well, if you won't bring it up⁷, then perhaps we should recommend a dress code⁸ at the next teachers' meeting!
Mr. Lee:	No, I mean, that's not necessary. I mean, I hope that we can work this out.

CHECK YOUR UNDERSTANDING

1. What do the students think of Ms. Bailey?

....

2. What does Ms. Rios think of Ms. Bailey?

....

3. What does Ms. Rios propose to do about the situation?

....

4. Does Mr. Lee agree with Ms. Rios?

....

Read these three opinions.

Carmen

Ms. Rios was wrong to complain about how another teacher dresses.

Ray

Mr. Lee should tell Ms. Bailey to dress differently.

Amber

Mr. Lee should talk to some of the students to see if there is a problem.

Match the supporting statements with the opinions. Write the numbers in the boxes.
Each opinion has two supporting statements.

supporting statements

1

It is the job of the school director to make sure that teachers act and dress correctly.

2

If you have a problem with someone, talk directly to that person.

3

The director of a school needs to make sure that students pay attention to their studies.

4

Perhaps Ms. Rios is the only person who is upset by the way Ms. Bailey dresses.

5

We should not act quickly. We need to think before we act.

6

Don't worry about what other people do. Just do the best job that you can do.

Now compare with a classmate.

Work in a group of three. Ask your partners:
Do you agree with Carmen? Do you agree with Ray? Do you agree with Amber?
Answer for each person: *I really agree / I agree / I disagree / I really disagree.*

WHAT ARE YOUR VALUES?

What should Mr. Lee do? State your position and support your ideas.
Use new ideas in addition to the ideas above.

Your Position

Supporting Statements

CLARIFYING & EXCHANGING

Now form groups and discuss your position and supporting statements.

DISCUSSION ACTIVITY

Describe what you would wear in these situations. Give a reason:

Situation	Clothes	Reason
To school:		
To work:		
To the movies:		
To an expensive restaurant:		
To a wedding:		
To a funeral:		
To a job interview:		
your idea:		

Now compare your ideas with a partner.

17 A Chocolate Lover's Nightmare

VALUES in the WORKPLACE

WARM UP

1. Have you ever done something embarrassing at work or at school?

2. Have you ever done something to make your boss angry?

3. What is the most irresistible food in the world for you?

SITUATION

🎧 **Sometimes a small act can cause a big problem. In this story, Lydia is in trouble. Why?**

What does she decide to do next?

I'm in chocolate trouble! Last week our boss came back from Europe and brought some Belgian chocolate into the office. At lunch, when I went to the employee refrigerator[1] to get my lunch, I saw the box in there, and I knew it was for us! But for the rest of the day, my boss didn't say anything. I kept checking the refrigerator, and back at my desk, I couldn't stop thinking of the chocolate.

Then, around 4:00, I pretended[2] to go for coffee, but in fact I went to the employees' lounge and took out the box of chocolates. I was only going to smell it. But when I had it in my hands I thought, "It's okay, it's for us. Why not have my piece a little early?" So I opened it up and ate one and went back to my desk.

A bit later, I found myself back at the refrigerator. I looked at the box and noticed that you couldn't tell one was missing. The box still looked full. I thought, "I might as well[3] have a second piece." It was so good. I was in heaven[4]. Then I thought, "Well, three isn't so different from two... well, four isn't so different from three..." until suddenly I had eaten half the box. I felt really stupid. I knew that I'd have to admit that I ate all of those chocolates. But, oh well — what's done is done. I closed the box and retied[5] the ribbon and thought, "At least it looks okay from the outside."

The explosion[6] came the next day. The chocolates were for a client[7]. When the client opened the box and it was half empty, my boss nearly died of embarrassment[8]. That was a week ago. Our boss is still furious[9] and has been making everyone work late. She keeps asking us over and over who ate the chocolates. She says she told everyone beforehand that they were for a client. My colleagues[10] are disgusted[11] with her attitude, but are also disgusted that "the thief" hasn't admitted to the crime. I think that they secretly suspect me. I never thought this problem would get so big. Should I quit my job? Admit the truth? Just let things calm down? I'm in so much trouble.

CHECK YOUR UNDERSTANDING

1. What did Lydia do that got her in trouble?

....

2. What was her boss's reaction?

....

3. What is Lydia's main problem?

....

4. What are Lydia's choices now?

....

POINTS OF VIEW

Read these three opinions.

James

Lydia should admit to her boss that she stole the chocolate.

Anton

Lydia should tell the truth to her co-workers and ask for advice.

Carmen

It is better if Lydia doesn't tell anyone.

Match the supporting statements with the opinions. Write the numbers in the boxes.
Each opinion has two supporting statements.

supporting statements

1
It's unfair to make her co-workers suffer.

2
There's nothing to be gained, and a lot to lose.

3
They can help decide how to handle the situation.

4
If you make a mistake, you should be honest about it.

5
Her co-workers have a right to know.

6
Admitting a mistake would only make things worse.

Now compare with a classmate.

Work in a group of three. Ask your partners:
Do you agree with James? Do you agree with Anton? Do you agree with Carmen?
Answer for each person: *I really agree / I agree / I disagree / I really disagree.*

WHAT ARE YOUR VALUES?

What would you do in this situation? State your position and support your ideas.
Use new ideas in addition to the ideas above.

Your Position

Supporting Statements

CLARIFYING & EXCHANGING

Now form groups and discuss your position and supporting statements.

PERSONAL STORY

Tell a story about a time you felt embarrassed. Draw simple pictures in these four squares to show what happened. Tell the story using the language below.

language

I remember once...
When I was... years old
In this picture here, I...
This is a picture of...
Then what happened was...
Next...
After that...
I felt... horrible/ totally embarrassed/ shocked

18 Career Choice

WARM UP

1. What's more important, money or free time?

2. Is status important to you?

3. What kind of company would you like to work for?

SITUATION 🎧 **Ted and Ken are good friends. They have just graduated from university. Ted has been offered two jobs. Which job will he take? Why?**

Ken: So, how's your job search going?

Ted: Great. You won't believe this — I got a job offer from Wastrix! Oh, and one from Econotron, too.

Ken: Wastrix or Econotron? Wow, well, that should be an easy decision.

Ted: Yeah. I'm taking the Wastrix offer.

Ken: You're kidding[1], right?

Ted: No. I'd be crazy to say no to Wastrix. They're a top company. I might never get an offer like this again.

Ken: Wastrix has such a bad reputation[2]. You know, the long hours... the stress...

Ted: Think about the money, though. The salary they're offering me is 30% higher than Econotron! It'll be worth a little extra stress.

Ken: I don't know. You might burn out[3]. In a few years, you'll hate your life.

Ted: I have to at least give it a shot[4]. It's Wastrix! They're the biggest company in my field.

Ken: You're not even going to think about the Econotron offer?

Ted: Why should I?

Ken: Well, I'll tell you why. A lot less overtime, a less competitive atmosphere[5]. I've heard it's a very creative place to work.

Ted: Oh, a creative place to work? Come on, that's just naive.

Ken: Well, think about the environment, then. Wastrix makes all those toxic[6] chemicals, and they have all those lawsuits[7] about polluting the environment. Econotron is, you know, a much more environmentally friendly[8] company.

Ted: Now you're really being naive[9]. I don't believe all of that stuff about Econotron. I think they're just saying they're environmentally friendly. Look, I just have to take the job that's going to help me get ahead.

Ken: I don't know. It just might be a mistake.

Ted: Hey, talk to me in a couple of years when I'm giving you a ride in my Mercedes.

CHECK YOUR UNDERSTANDING

1. What kind of company is Wastrix? ....

2. What kind of company is Econotron? ....

3. What does Ted think is important for his career? ....

4. What does Ken think Ted should do? ....

Read these three opinions.

Pablo

Ken is being unrealistic. Ted will be happy at Wastrix.

Carmen

Ted is making a mistake. He will be unhappy in the future.

Koji

Ted should go to Wastrix and try to help the company improve.

Match the supporting statements with the opinions. Write the numbers in the boxes.
Each opinion has two supporting statements.

supporting statements

1

It's possible to change things if we try hard.

2

The world is a competitive place.

3

We have to take advantage of every opportunity we get.

4

Money doesn't make happiness.

5

It's possible to have success and also follow your ideals.

6

A good lifestyle is more important than status.

Now compare with a classmate.

Work in a group of three. Ask your partners:
Do you agree with Pablo? Do you agree with Carmen? Do you agree with Koji?
Answer for each person: *I really agree / I agree / I disagree / I really disagree.*

WHAT ARE YOUR VALUES?

Are you an idealist about your career? A realist? State your position and support your ideas.
Use new ideas in addition to the ideas above.

Your Position

Supporting Statements

CLARIFYING & EXCHANGING

Now form groups and discuss your position and supporting statements.

DISCUSSION ACTIVITY

What's your dream career? What are the good and bad points of the following careers?
Discuss with your partner.

- music industry
- multinational corporation
- fashion world
- engineering
- sports
- entertainment

example
A: What are the good points of working in the music industry?
B: Well, you can make a lot of money, and get to meet creative people.
A: How about the bad points?
B: You have a crazy schedule. And it's a competitive business...

V A L U E S in the FAMILY

In this section, people share their opinions about how to solve different kinds of family conflicts.

19 Following Him

Is it okay for parents to ask their children to give up something important for them?

If you are in a serious relationship, how important is your partner's family?

A man's family asks him to make a difficult decision.

20 A Mother's Worry

Should both parents share the job of taking care of children?

Is it okay for both parents of young children to work?

A mother feels torn between working and taking care of her son.

21 A Good Parent

Can anyone be a parent?

What does it take to be a good parent?

A man explains why he thinks his parents are good parents.

22 Losing Touch

What are some good things about a bicultural family?

What are some bad things?

A bicultural couple discusses their daughter's future plan.

23 A Daughter's Decision

Is abortion ever okay?

If a teenager wants an abortion, what should the parents do?

An 18-year-old girl wants an abortion.
Her parents try to decide what to say to her.

24 Whose Child?

What are some advances in medical technology?

What do you think of "surrogate motherhood"?

Three women share their views on surrogate motherhood.

19 Following Him

WARM UP

1. Have you ever said "no" to your mother or father?
2. Do you want to live close to your family?
3. Would you move far away from your family for love?

SITUATION ∩ **Kyle and Lyn are planning to get married in three months, but they have a problem. Kyle's family wants him to move back to his small hometown. Why does his family want him to move back?**

Kyle: Hello.
Lyn: Hi, Kyle.
Kyle: Hey.
Lyn: How are you?
Kyle: Great.
Lyn: How's your father doing? Is he getting better?
Kyle: Uh, Lyn, I was just going to call you. We've got to talk.
Lyn: Kyle, we... we can talk when you get back.
Kyle: Well, Lyn...
Lyn: When are you coming back? I miss you.
Kyle: I miss you, too. But, but I'm not really sure, you see. It's difficult.
Lyn: What do you mean?
Kyle: Well, my... my father's getting better.
Lyn: Oh, that's good.
Kyle: Yeah. Yeah. But he's still very weak, and he won't be able to go back to work for a long time.
Lyn: Oh.
Kyle: He... he wants me to stay here and... and work in the family hotel.
Lyn: What? Work in the hotel?
Kyle: Yeah.
Lyn: Like, permanently[1]?
Kyle: Well, Lyn, my... my family really wants me to live here. In fact, I was thinking. I wanted to ask you — how would you feel about moving here?
Lyn: Ah–

Kyle: I know, I know. It's a small town, but really, it's a wonderful place and it's a great place to live and... and have a family.
Lyn: Kyle, you're not serious! How can you ask me to leave the city? All my friends, my family are all here.
Kyle: I know.
Lyn: I have such better job opportunities[2]. My whole life is here. What about your job?
Kyle: I know, I know. If I stay here, then I'll have to quit[3] my job and... and just work in the hotel. But my family, they need me here.

Lyn: What about me?
Kyle: I love you, Lyn. I know... I know this is really hard, and we weren't expecting it, but I want us to be together. Both of us, here. It won't be forever.
Lyn: I don't know, Kyle. I don't know. I... I just can't see myself being happy there. I love you, I really do, but I don't want to live there. I know I would be really unhappy.

CHECK YOUR UNDERSTANDING

1. What happened to Kyle's father?
....
2. Does Kyle want to go back?
....
3. How does Lyn feel about the situation?
....

Read these three opinions.

Monica

Kyle should say "no" to his family, and stay with Lyn.

Ray

Lyn should go with Kyle back to his hometown.

Trin

Kyle should return to his hometown, even if Lyn won't go.

Match the supporting statements with the opinions. Write the numbers in the boxes.
Each opinion has two supporting statements.

s u p p o r t i n g   s t a t e m e n t s

1

We sometimes have to sacrifice now in order to be happy later.

2

We shouldn't give up our future just to please others.

3

If we really disagree with our family's request, we shouldn't follow it.

4

Life has many ups and downs, but a family is forever.

5

We owe everything to our parents, so we have to help them.

6

If we always insist on getting what we want, we will never be happy.

Now compare with a classmate.

Work in a group of three. Ask your partners:
Do you agree with Monica? Do you agree with Ray? Do you agree with Trin?
Answer for each person: *I really agree / I agree / I disagree / I really disagree.*

WHAT ARE YOUR VALUES?

What should Kyle and Lyn do? Write your advice and your reasons.
Use new ideas in addition to the ideas above.

Advice

Reasons

CLARIFYING & EXCHANGING

Now form groups and discuss your advice and reasons.

PERSONAL STORY

Tell a story about an experience that made you a better person. Follow these steps:
Brainstorming – Think of topics you could talk about (make notes).
Preparation – Organize your ideas (outline or written story).
Presentation – Read or tell your story to classmates.

....

....

....

20 | A Mother's Worry

WARM UP

1. What do you think about mothers who use day care for young children?

2. What age is okay for children to start day care?

3. Are mothers better parents than fathers?

SITUATION ∩ **Margarita is a mother with a three-year-old son, Marcos. She recently returned to doing design work at her old company, but she has a problem. What is bothering her?**

Hi, Rosa,

Sorry it's been so long since I emailed you. I've been very busy since I returned to work. Do you remember that two months ago I decided that Marcos was old enough to be more independent[1]? I think I emailed you that I put him in a child-care center[2] and went back to my old job at the advertising agency[3].

Now I need to ask your opinion about something. You know that three years ago when Marcos was born I quit my job. At the time, I thought it was best. But you know me. I loved my work, and my company always said I could come back whenever I wanted to.

Do you remember how difficult it was for me to convince my husband? Raul is so traditional[4]. He worries about Marcos. Raul works a lot and can't help me that much. He also says that children should be with their mothers as much as possible. But finally he agreed because, after all, he wants me to be happy.

It's been fun. I like my job and my co-workers[5]. But there's a problem. It's been harder than I expected. Raul has started to complain. He tries to help, but he can't cook and he hates housework. Of course, he thinks he's being a perfect husband. Marcos gets sick sometimes at the child-care center. So I have to leave work early to take him to the doctor or home. To tell the truth, I'm really stressed. When I finally get home after work, I'm exhausted[6].

Even though it's been harder than I expected, my job is very important to me. I know that I cannot be only a mother and a housewife. At the same time, as a mother, Marcos is also very important to me. The teacher at the child-care center said that Marcos seems fine. She said that being with other kids is good for him. Maybe so, but I'm not sure if I'm doing the right thing.

What do you think? I can always depend on you for good advice. I hope everything is fine with you.
Take care,

Margarita

CHECK YOUR UNDERSTANDING

1. Why did Margarita decide to put her son in a day-care center? ....
2. What is causing Margarita's stress? ....
3. How does Raul feel about the situation? ....

Read these three opinions.

Anton

Margarita should work part-time. ▢ ▢

Amber

She should keep working full-time and try to get support from her husband. ▢ ▢

Trin

Margarita should not work. She needs to be a full-time mother. ▢ ▢

Match the supporting statements with the opinions. Write the numbers in the boxes.
Each opinion has two supporting statements.

s u p p o r t i n g s t a t e m e n t s

1

It's just not possible to combine work with being a mother.

2

A mother needs to be happy with her life to be a good mother.

3

A truly happy family needs some-one at home full time.

4

Husbands and wives need to coop-erate and solve problems together.

5

Young children are very flexible. They don't need a full-time mother.

6

It is necessary to have a balance in your life.

Now compare with a classmate.

Work in a group of three. Ask your partners:
Do you agree with Anton? Do you agree with Amber? Do you agree with Trin?
Answer for each person: *I really agree / I agree / I disagree / I really disagree.*

What advice would you give to Margarita? Write your advice and your reasons.
Use new ideas in addition to the ideas above.

Your Position ▶ **Supporting Statements** ▶

Now form groups and discuss your position and supporting statements.

Gender stereotypes

What is the most common image of "woman" and "man" in your culture?
Write "M" next to the words which have a male image for you. Write "F" for words with a female image. Write "M / F" for words that seem equally male and female.

.... logical .... serious .... creative .... sensitive
.... caring .... emotional .... hard-working .... strong

Look at your partner's answers, and compare them with your own. Ask your partner about his or her answers.

21 | A Good Parent

1. Do you know anyone who is an adopted child? What do they think about it?

2. Who should be allowed to adopt a child?

SITUATION

🎧 **Darren is talking about his parents and his relationship to them. What is different about Darren's parents?**

You know how people always ask you about your family... how many brothers and sisters do you have, what do your parents do, questions like that?

Well, when I tell people about my family, most of the time, they don't believe me.

You see, I'm adopted¹. Now, that's not the hard thing to believe. A lot of people are adopted. What's different is my parents. I don't have your traditional² mother and father. I have two fathers. I was adopted by two men, a gay³ couple. My two fathers are the only parents I've ever known.

My parents are great. Really open, really supportive⁴. I've always been able to talk to them about important things — school, sports, friends, problems I'm having. And now that I'm in college and live away from home, we still talk on the phone all the time. They're really easy to talk to. I don't have to hide things like some of my friends have to hide from their parents.

Okay, I know exactly what you're thinking. You're thinking, "Someone with two gay fathers must be gay, right?" Well, actually, I'm not. And, no, my... my parents aren't disappointed⁵. They accept me just the way I am. They've even met my girlfriend, Denise, and they think she's great.

It hasn't always been easy, though. Once, when I was about twelve, I invited a friend, a guy named Rick, over to my house. When Rick met my two fathers, he didn't say anything. But later, Rick's parents told him that he wasn't allowed⁶ to be friends with me anymore. They said I wasn't a "good influence"⁷ on their son. Even worse, they called my school. They complained about⁸ my parents, and said my parents were corrupting⁹ the kids. For no reason. Well, to make a long story short... I actually ended up leaving that school and going over to a new one.

I don't regret¹⁰ any of the hard times, though. They've taught me a lot about life, and I've learned that I can really count on¹¹ my parents.

You know, people ask what it takes to be a good parent, and I'll tell you: being a good parent has nothing to do with gender¹². It's all about love.

CHECK YOUR UNDERSTANDING

1. What is Darren's relationship with his parents like? ....
2. What do Darren's parents think about Darren's girlfriend? ....
3. According to Darren, what makes a good parent? ....

Read these three opinions.

Trin

Whenever possible, children should be brought up by their birth parents. ▢ ▢

Monica

Love is what makes a good family. ▢ ▢

Koji

Children brought up by same-gender parents will have many problems in society. ▢ ▢

Match the supporting statements with the opinions. Write the numbers in the boxes.
Each opinion has two supporting statements.

supporting statements

1

Human societies have always been built on the traditional family—a mother, father, and their children.

2

Even if their parents love the child, other children will not accept them and will treat them badly.

3

These children will not be able to overcome social pressure and prejudice.

4

Same-gender couples are like anyone else: they can be very loving parents.

5

Children need to know where they come from. They get their identity and sense of gender from their parents.

6

Parents for orphans are needed. Gender does not matter.

Now compare with a classmate.

Work in a group of three. Ask your partners:
Do you agree with Trin? Do you agree with Monica? Do you agree with Koji?
Answer for each person: *I really agree / I agree / I disagree / I really disagree.*

WHAT ARE YOUR VALUES?

What do you think about same-gender parents? State your position and support your ideas.
Use new ideas in addition to the ideas above.

Your Position ▶ **Supporting Statements** ▶

> ### CLARIFYING & EXCHANGING
> **Now form groups and discuss your position and supporting statements.**

VALUES EXCHANGE

What are the most important qualities of a good family? Choose the three values that are the most important.
A good family...

.... always does things together
.... helps each other
.... is always kind to each other
.... talks together about problems

.... makes sacrifices for each other
.... enjoys being together
.... protects each other from difficulties
your own idea: ....

Compare with a partner.

22

Losing Touch

WARM UP

1. Is your cultural identity important to you?

2. Would you marry someone from a different country?

3. Could you raise your family in a different country?

4. Do you know anyone who was raised in a different country than his or her parents?

SITUATION

🎧 **Rozenn is 14. She grew up in Canada with her Canadian father and Brazilian mother. Every year she spends her summer vacation with her relatives in Brazil, but this year she doesn't want to. What will her parents decide?**

Philip: Honey, I think we need to talk about Rozenn's plans for the summer. I mean, I know you feel strongly about Rozenn staying in touch with[1] your family, but I think we should let her stay here in Canada during the summer. She has band practice and the school summer camp.

Ana: Phillip, my parents would be crushed[2] if Rozenn didn't go back to Brazil. And you know that's their only chance to see her.

Philip: Well, I know that, but I'm just not sure we should make her go just because your parents want to see her.

Ana: Oh, it's more than that. Also, she's losing her Portuguese. She needs to keep it up, or she'll never get it back.

Philip: Well, I know that's important to you, but she's had some trouble making friends in school, and the fact that she wants to be with them now is a good thing.

Ana: But she always has fun when she goes to Brazil. It's for her own good. And honey, remember when she was born, we promised to raise her biculturally[3].

Philip: And we have done that. But she's 14, and she wants to be her own person. She can go next year.

Ana: She won't want to go. Honey, you don't know what it's like to leave your country, and your family. If Rozenn loses touch with[4] Brazil, she's losing touch with me.

Philip: Well, I know she'll do whatever we decide, but at her age I just don't like telling her what to do.

Ana: Yes, she's a good girl. But you also know that she sometimes likes to take the easy way out. It'll be better if she goes. She'll thank us in the end[5].

CHECK YOUR UNDERSTANDING

1. Why does Philip think Rozenn should stay in Canada? ....

2. Why does Ana think Rozenn should go to Brazil?..

3. What do you think Rozenn wants to do? ....

Read these three opinions.

Pablo

They should have her spend the summer in Brazil.

Carmen

They should let her stay in Canada with her friends.

Ray

They should explain their concerns to her, and then let her decide.

Match the supporting statements with the opinions. Write the numbers in the boxes.
Each opinion has two supporting statements.

supporting statements

1

Being with her friends is fun, but biculturalism is more important.

2

She's old enough to make her own choices.

3

If her parents can't agree, the child should decide.

4

Forcing someone to do something never brings good results.

5

Nothing can replace one's culture, heritage, and family.

6

Her friends in Canada are just as important as her family in Brazil.

Now compare with a classmate.

Work in a group of three. Ask your partners:
Do you agree with Pablo? Do you agree with Carmen? Do you agree with Ray?
Answer for each person: *I really agree / I agree / I disagree / I really disagree.*

What should Philip and Ana do about Rozenn? State your position and support your ideas.
Use new ideas in addition to the ideas above.

Your Position	Supporting Statements	CLARIFYING & EXCHANGING
		Now form groups and discuss your position and supporting statements.

How do you develop an "identity" with another culture? Check the five most important things.

.... learning dances from that culture
.... learning the language
.... preparing food from that culture
.... eating the food
.... wearing the clothes they wear
.... talking to people from the culture
.... going to museums with exhibits about that culture

.... visiting there
.... living there
.... having friends from there
.... marrying someone from there
.... adopting the religion of that culture
.... reading books by authors from that culture
.... following the customs of that culture

Compare your list with your partner. Explain your reasons.

your reasons ....

A Daughter's Decision

WARM UP

1. Is abortion legal in your country?

a. Yes. A woman can have an abortion. **b.** Yes, but only in certain situations. (What are they?)
c. No, never.

SITUATION

🎧 **Roy and Martha Brown have an 18-year-old daughter, Jan. What does Jan want to do? How do Roy and Martha feel?**

Martha: Okay, honey, well, I think we need to talk about this some more. Yes, let's talk tomorrow. Bye, I love you, too.

Roy: Was that Jan?

Martha: Yeah.

Roy: What's the trouble this time?

Martha: I just found out. Jan's pregnant[1]. She wants to have an abortion[2].

Roy: That's... that's terrible. You know, I had a feeling something like this was going to happen. What did you tell her?

Martha: Well, you know where I stand—I told her that she shouldn't go through with it[3]. She can't have an abortion. We have to convince[4] her to change her mind.

Roy: I'm... I'm not with you[5] on this one, honey. I think Jan is right.

Martha: You can't be serious! You think she should get an abortion? Don't you remember? That's what everyone told me when I was eighteen. "Get an abortion. You're too young to have a baby. It'll ruin[6] your life." But I didn't. And I thought you agreed with me.

Roy: Well, I... I did! Then. But that was you. You were amazing[7]. You could handle[8] it. You knew what you were doing. And I was there to support you and help you raise[9] the baby. With Jan, it's completely different. She's not responsible[10] enough to have a baby. And she can't take care of it. Look at all of the trouble she's having just taking care of herself. And she doesn't want to be a mother.

Martha: She's just saying that now because she's scared[11]. We have to show her that things will be all right. We'll help her. And being a mother teaches responsibility[12]. Jan will do fine if she has our support.

Roy: But this won't teach Jan responsibility. You know, honey, sometimes I think... I just think abortion is the right thing to do.

Martha: I don't believe that. You know that. We need to make her see that abortion is always a terrible mistake. She'll regret it for the rest of her life if she goes through with it, don't you see?

Roy: I don't know if it is a mistake for Jan. I just... I just don't know.

Martha: Roy, this is something that a man simply can't understand.

CHECK YOUR UNDERSTANDING

1. What does Martha want Jan to do? Why?

....

2. What does Roy want Jan to do? Why?

....

3. How are Martha and Jan similar?

....

Read these three opinions.

Carmen

Martha and Roy should allow Jan to have an abortion.

Anton

Martha and Roy should encourage Jan to have the child and give it up for adoption.

Koji

Martha and Roy should encourage Jan to have the child and raise it.

Match the supporting statements with the opinions. Write the numbers in the boxes.
Each opinion has two supporting statements.

supporting statements

1

Once the baby is born, she will love it.

2

Abortion is too extreme. We can always give up the baby to a couple who want the child.

3

An unmarried woman may not be able to take care of a baby by herself.

4

Unwanted children create problems for everyone.

5

Abortion is not an answer. We must live with the consequences of our actions.

6

A grown woman should be able to make her own decisions.

Now compare with a classmate.

Work in a group of three. Ask your partners:
Do you agree with Carmen? Do you agree with Anton? Do you agree with Koji?
Answer for each person: *I really agree / I agree / I disagree / I really disagree.*

WHAT ARE YOUR VALUES?

What do you think Jan should do? Give your advice and your reasons.
Use new ideas in addition to the ideas above.

Advice	Reasons	CLARIFYING & EXCHANGING
		Now form groups and discuss your advice and reasons.

PERSONAL STORY

Tell a story about an experience in which you followed the advice of a parent or close relative or friend.
Follow these steps:

Brainstorming – Think of experiences you could talk about (make notes).
Preparation – Organize your ideas (outline or written story).
Presentation – Read or tell your story to classmates.

....
....
....

24 | Whose Child?

WARM UP

1. If you are a woman, do you want to be a mother?

2. If you are a man, do you want to be married and have children?

3. If you couldn't have children, what would you do?

SITUATION

🎧 **A surrogate mother is a woman who is paid to have another couple's child. Here are three women's opinions about surrogate mothers.**

What is the process of being a surrogate mother?

What kinds of problems can occur?

Lisa: What do I think about being a surrogate mother? Let me tell you my story.

Three years ago, I had a baby girl, Stephanie. She was so beautiful, and when I think about her, I know how happy her parents are. Max and Betty wanted a child so badly, and this was the only way they could have their own child. I was so happy to help. It's so exciting to make a family for someone else. I know how wonderful motherhood¹ is — I have two lovely kids of my own — and I wanted to share this with other people. I think more people should be surrogate mothers. It's a wonderful way to give life to others.

Ann: What do I think of surrogate motherhood? Let me tell you what happened to me and my husband.

We are so sad. Our baby, Theodore, was born two weeks ago, and we had everything ready for him: the crib², the clothes, the toys, and our hearts were ready for him to come home. But now we can't even hold him in our arms. It's so cruel³. It's because that... that woman, the surrogate mother, refuses⁴ to give us our baby. It's our baby. She agreed to give us the baby as soon as it was born. We already signed a contract⁵, and already paid her a lot of money, and we were prepared to pay her the rest... when she changed her mind. Now she says she wants to keep Theodore and she doesn't want the money. She says that she loves him, and she can't give him up. But she couldn't love him as much as we do. He's our baby! It's my egg⁶ that was fertilized⁷ with my husband's sperm⁸ in the test tube. So Theodore has our DNA, not hers. This is all difficult and expensive. She has no right to take away our baby.

CHECK YOUR UNDERSTANDING

1. What is Lisa's opinion about surrogate motherhood?

....

2. What was Ann's experience with surrogate motherhood?

....

3. What happened to Maria?

....

Maria: What do I think of being a surrogate mother? Well, let me tell you my story.

I had a baby six months ago, little Brian. He was supposed to go to a young couple who couldn't have their own children, so they hired me, and they paid me really well. But, unfortunately Brian was born prematurely⁹, and because he was so small when he was born and he was born so early, he had heart problems. Oh, he was so cute, but, with all of these heart problems, the couple decided that they didn't want him. They said the contract was for a healthy baby. So, I decided to keep him. I... I couldn't put him up for adoption¹⁰. I'd had him. But so far, he's had three operations. He's getting better, but the doctors say that he'll still need operations when he's older. And I love him. I'm... I'm really happy to be his mother, but I'm really worried. I may not be able to afford¹¹ to keep him.

Read these three opinions.

Pablo

Test-tube babies and surrogate mothers are important advances in our society. ▢ ▢

Monica

Test-tube babies and surrogate mothers are unnatural. ▢ ▢

James

Having children is not everything in life. ▢ ▢

Match the supporting statements with the opinions. Write the numbers in the boxes.
Each opinion has two supporting statements.

supporting statements

1

Unnatural pregnancy or childbirth is too risky. It's not clear who is responsible when there is a problem.

2

It's not essential for all couples to have children. The world is overpopulated anyway.

3

People who want babies should be able to use the newest technologies available.

4

Let's not make our life too complicated. Traditional childbirth is the best.

5

Some people really want their own babies. We should understand that.

6

If you can't have your own baby, think about adoption. There are so many babies who need parents in this world.

Now compare with a classmate.

Work in a group of three. Ask your partners:
Do you agree with Pablo? Do you agree with Monica? Do you agree with James?
Answer for each person: *I really agree / I agree / I disagree / I really disagree.*

WHAT ARE YOUR VALUES?

Is surrogate motherhood okay? State your position and support your ideas.
Use new ideas in addition to the ideas above.

Your Position →

Supporting Statements →

CLARIFYING & EXCHANGING

Now form groups and discuss your position and supporting statements.

VALUES DEBATE

Predict and debate. Will surrogate motherhood be a big business in the future?
Split pairs or groups into two sides, "Yes" and "No". Take time to write down your ideas, and how you will answer the points of the other side. Set a time limit and debate! Use the language below.

My ideas
....
....
....
....
....

language
Yes, it will. No, it won't.
Technology will keep developing, so it will be safer.
When there is a choice, people will take it.
It will be against the law.
Many people feel it's too unnatural.
It shouldn't be a business.

V A L U E S in S O C I E T Y

In this section you'll get a chance to discuss important
global issues.

25 Saving Mother Earth

Is the earth in crisis?

How important is the environment?

An author discusses the Earth's
environmental problems.

26 Aging Parent

Who should take care of the elderly?

What is the best place for an elderly
person to live?

A landlord wants his elderly tenant to
find a new home.

27 Can War Make Peace?

Is war ever justified? If so, when?

A boy wonders if war is ever the right
way to solve the world's problems.

28 Do Animals Have Rights?

Are animals on earth to help humans?

Is it okay to experiment with animals?

An animal rights activist and a research scientist debate the roles animals should play in our lives.

29 A Way to Escape

How does alcohol cause problems for people?

What should we do if drinking gets a friend in trouble?

A boy wonders how to help his friend.

30 Adult Children

Should adults be independent from their families?

When do people become adults?

Two experts talk about the phenomenon of grown children living at home.

WARM UP
1. What things in modern life are "convenient" for you?
2. Would you be willing to give up convenience for the environment?
3. Have you been doing anything to solve environmental problems?

SITUATION ∩ *Hot Seat* is an interview program about current, controversial issues. Today's topic is the environment. What is the guest's main point?

Interviewer: Welcome to *Hot Seat,* the interview show with tough[1] talk and tough questions. Today we're with John Sanders, best-selling author[2] of a controversial[3] new book: *Give Up Convenience, Save Mother Earth.* Welcome to our program.

Mr. Sanders: I'm happy to be here.

Interviewer: Now, in your book, you say that we will be hated by future generations[4] for not saving "Mother Earth." Is that right?

Mr. Sanders: Yes. We're in crisis[5], and it's a result of our selfishness. We're killing our own mother for a tiny bit of convenience.

Interviewer: Killing our own mother?

Mr. Sanders: We consume[6], we waste, and we think it's all natural. We understand this pace of development is damaging the Earth, but we can't give up our cars, our convenience stores.

Interviewer: Yes, right. In your book you criticize convenience stores.

Mr. Sanders: That's right. Think of all the electricity used for the bright lights, heating food and cooling drinks all day and all night. We pull oil from the ground — burn it to make electricity, produce CO_2,[7] cause global warming. For what? For a lifestyle that ruins our health

Give up Convenience, Save Mother Earth

John Sanders

and our environment. And we're doing nothing about it.

Interviewer: Well, do I remember correctly? Last month in Brussels there was a United Nations conference on —

Mr. Sanders: Meaningless. People are slaves to a convenience-store lifestyle. Everyone knows it, but no one has the courage[8] to change. I, for example, never use plastics. I grow my own chemical-free[9] vegetables, always take public transportation[10]—

Interviewer: That's not practical[11]. To be honest, it sounds like you're just trying to sell your books.

Mr. Sanders: Not at all. To change this, everyone, and I mean EVERYONE, needs to give up some convenience from their lives. Start simple. No more plastic bottles. Refuse to drink from anything except glass. Until you give something up, nothing will change.

Interviewer: Oh, come on, the problems of the world are not going to be solved by me drinking from a glass.

Mr. Sanders: All right. There are many other things you can do.

Interviewer: Yeah.

Mr. Sanders: You'll find more ideas in my book, *Give Up Convenience, Save Mother Earth.* It's available[12] in every bookstore.

CHECK YOUR UNDERSTANDING

1. What is Mr. Sanders' problem with modern lifestyles?
....
2. What does Mr. Sanders believe we should give up?
....
3. Why does the interviewer challenge Mr. Sanders?
....

POINTS OF VIEW Read these three opinions.

Pablo

Mr. Sanders is right. We should give up a lot of convenience in order to save the Earth.

Ray

Mr. Sanders may be right, but his ideas for solving the problems are not realistic.

Carmen

Mr. Sanders is simply appealing to our emotions in order to sell books.

Match the supporting statements with the opinions. Write the numbers in the boxes.
Each opinion has two supporting statements.

supporting statements

1

People have been saying things like this for years. Our environmental problems are not so serious.

2

What we really need is more action from government.

3

We all know that things like plastics and automobiles damage the environment.

4

The root of these problems is economic. No one will change as long as things are cheap.

5

We should change our lifestyle in order to protect our Earth.

6

He is only telling one side of the story to make us believe him. He ignores the fact that modern technology helps humankind.

Now compare with a classmate.

Work in a group of three. Ask your partners:
Do you agree with Pablo? Do you agree with Ray? Do you agree with Carmen?
Answer for each person: *I really agree / I agree / I disagree / I really disagree.*

WHAT ARE YOUR VALUES?

Is the environment in crisis? State your position and support your ideas.
Use new ideas in addition to the ideas above.

Your Position ▶ **Supporting Statements** ▶

CLARIFYING & EXCHANGING

Now form groups and discuss your position and supporting statements.

VALUES EXCHANGE

Which of these things would you give up to save the environment?

Yes Maybe No
.... Tissues
.... Plastic bottles
.... Disposable chopsticks
.... Your car

Yes Maybe No
.... Shopping at convenience stores
.... Air conditioners in your house
your own idea: ....

example
A: Would you give up tissues?   B: Well, maybe, but I don't know what else I can use.

Interview your partner. Ask what she or he will give up and why.

25

26 | Aging Parent

WARM UP

1. Do you have grandparents or old parents? Who takes care of them?

2. When you are 80 years old, where do you think you will live?

3. How does the government take care of old people in your area or country?

SITUATION ∩ **Shawn's mother, Andrea, lives by herself in an apartment close to Shawn. Shawn stops to talk to her landlord. The landlord, Mr. Jensen, wants Andrea to move out of the apartment. Why does Mr. Jensen want Shawn's mother to move? How does Shawn react?**

Shawn: Mr. Jensen, here's my mother's rent.

Mr. Jensen: Yes, thanks. But wait, there's something I need to bring up with you.

Shawn: Oh? What is it? Is there a problem?

Mr. Jensen: To be honest, yes.

Shawn: What's the problem?

Mr. Jensen: I'm just... I'm not comfortable with your mother living in the apartment anymore.

Shawn: Why? She's a great tenant[1]. She's quiet, I always pay her rent on time.

Mr. Jensen: I... I know, but she's getting too...

Shawn: Too what?

Mr. Jensen: Too old. She's too old to live in the apartment by herself.

Shawn: But she's hardly ever alone. A helper comes in every morning, and my sister or I come every night. We always make sure she has everything she needs.

Mr. Jensen: Yeah. But, but you know, she's been here — what? five years now? And she keeps getting weaker and weaker. And then there was the accident.

Shawn: Okay, so she fell and broke her hip. That can happen to anyone! But she's better now. And she knows her limitations[2] now. She doesn't try to do everything by herself. Look, I'm telling you — we take care of her. You really don't need to worry about it.

Mr. Jensen: Look, I just don't want anybody to...

Shawn: To what?

Mr. Jensen: To die in my apartment.

Shawn: Hey, look, I think it's just old age that makes you nervous. You really don't have a right to kick her out on the street. Just because she's old.

Mr. Jensen: Actually, I do. The lease is coming up for renewal[3] next month. And I don't want her in for another whole year.

Shawn: But she has nowhere else to go!

Mr. Jensen: Why doesn't she live with you?

Shawn: No. She can't live with us. We don't have any room.

Mr. Jensen: Well, then, put her in a nursing home[4].

Shawn: Yeah, right! No, she'd never agree to that.

Mr. Jensen: Look, I can't wait for you to sort these things out. I want her out by the end of the month.

Shawn: The end of the month?! I... You... I can't believe this.

Mr. Jensen: I'm sorry, but I don't want any trouble. She's your mother. She's your responsibility[5], not mine.

CHECK YOUR UNDERSTANDING

1. What is Mr. Jensen afraid will happen to Shawn's mother?

....

2. What does Mr. Jensen ask Shawn to do?

....

3. Why does Shawn want his mother to stay in the apartment?

....

Read these three opinions.

Amber

The landlord is very unkind. He should let Shawn's mother stay in his apartment house. ▢

Koji

Shawn and his family should ask Shawn's mother to live with them again. ▢ ▢

James

The government should give more support to older people such as Shawn's mother. ▢ ▢

Match the supporting statements with the opinions. Write the numbers in the boxes.
Each opinion has two supporting statements.

supporting statements

1

Children are responsible for their parents, so they shouldn't try to get help from other people or the government.

2

Residents should have the right to live where they live now.

3

People in the community should be kind to old people.

4

Everyone — the family, the community, and the government — needs to help the elderly.

5

It is best for old parents to live with their children's family even if the house is small or there's a conflict.

6

There are many old people who can't get support from their family.

Now compare with a classmate.

Work in a group of three. Ask your partners:
Do you agree with Amber? Do you agree with Koji? Do you agree with James?
Answer for each person: *I really agree / I agree / I disagree / I really disagree.*

What should Shawn do? Write your advice and your reasons.
Use new ideas in addition to the ideas above.

Advice ▶ Reasons

CLARIFYING & EXCHANGING

Now form groups and discuss your advice and reasons.

What should a government do to support the aged? Circle yes or no for each idea.

Yes No Build nursing homes

Yes No Send helpers and nurses to homes to look after older people

Yes No Provide free medical care for people over 70 years old

Yes No Provide free equipment such as wheelchairs that older people need

Yes No Provide inexpensive housing for rent

Yes No Raise taxes in order to support the aged

your own ideas: ....

Compare with a partner. Which of the above services does your government already provide?

26

Can War Make Peace?

WARM UP

1. Has anybody in your family ever experienced war?

2. Do you think there will be no wars in this world some day?

3. What do you think causes war?

SITUATION 🎧 **This letter to the editor of a newspaper was written by 12-year-old Joshua. What does he think about war?**

I'm confused¹ these days. We are taught at home and at school that violence² is bad. For example, last week, my friend and I were playing at the beach. We found a really beautiful shell. My friend picked it up, but I saw it first, and I said it was mine. He said, no, it was his. I really wanted the shell, and I even thought about hitting him, that's how angry I was.

Now would that be right? No! I shouldn't use violence. I should talk with my friend instead, and come to an agreement³ with him that way. My parents and teachers often tell me that using violence is the least civilized⁴ way to solve problems.

So, if two adults had a disagreement, and if they used violence toward each other in order to win, is it all right? No! If one injured⁵ the other, they would be arrested⁶. If one killed the other, it's a murder⁷. They would be put into prison for years, possibly for the rest of their life.

Now, I'm confused. When two countries disagree, they often use violence. They fight a war. How come using violence is not okay at home, at school, or in your country but okay between countries?

So many people have been killed and injured because of wars. Not only soldiers but citizens, including small children and babies. And wars create refugees⁸, too — all over the world.

A war is extreme⁹ violence. Like two people fighting over a shell, just much bigger. Adults say they are fighting wars in order to solve problems and make peace. But can you really "make peace" by using violence and killing so many people?

I don't think so. I don't think that bombs and missiles can reach people's hearts and change them. Bombs and missiles can't create love and caring, and that's what we need in the world. Why do adults use violence so quickly? Why can't they use their wisdom¹⁰ and talk it over?

Adults might say that things are not that easy. But they are the ones that teach us to respect others, not to hurt people, and not to kill. Why are they contradicting¹¹ themselves? I want them to be our model.

CHECK YOUR UNDERSTANDING

1. What happened with Joshua and his friend? ....

2. What is Joshua confused about? ....

3. What does Joshua think is the key to peace? ....

4. What does Joshua want from adults? ....

Read these three opinions.

Trin

Joshua does not understand the real world.

Anton

In this case, the child is wiser than the adults.

Carmen

War is part of human society, now and forever.

Match the supporting statements with the opinions. Write the numbers in the boxes.
Each opinion has two supporting statements.

supporting statements

1
> Sometimes war is the only solution to an international problem.

2
> Fighting never solves anything in the long run.

3
> We can never change our animal instincts.

4
> There is no excuse for violence.

5
> As you get older, you understand that some people are fundamentally evil.

6
> Human history is full of wars.

Now compare with a classmate.

Work in a group of three. Ask your partners:
Do you agree with Trin? Do you agree with Anton? Do you agree with Carmen?
Answer for each person: *I really agree / I agree / I disagree / I really disagree.*

WHAT ARE YOUR VALUES?

Is war sometimes necessary? State your position and support your ideas.
Use new ideas in addition to the ideas above.

Your Position

Supporting Statements

CLARIFYING & EXCHANGING

Now form groups and discuss your position and supporting statements.

DEBATE ZONES

Read the following opinions on war and peace and circle *agree* or *disagree*.

1. If all countries owned nuclear weapons, there would be no war. agree disagree
2. There will be another world war someday. agree disagree
3. Peace will be gained by educating children. agree disagree
4. As long as humans keep producing deadly weapons, there will be wars. agree disagree
5. If women became leaders, the world would be more peaceful. agree disagree

Make an "agree" zone and a "disagree" zone in your classroom. Start with Opinion #1. Choose a zone. Stand in it. Line up and face the people in the opposite zone. Debate with the person across from you for two minutes. Continue with the other opinions.

Do Animals Have Rights?

1. Do you like animals? What are your favorite animals?
2. What role do animals play in our lives?
3. Could we live without animals?

SITUATION 🎧 *Animal World* is a talk show that discusses topics related to animals. What do today's speakers think about animal rights?

Moderator: Welcome to *Animal World*. Today's program is about Animal Rights[1]. Now, most of our viewers have already made up their minds about animal rights, but we have two guests here today to challenge our perspective[2]. Let's start with Dr. Faye. Could you introduce yourself and tell us what you do.

Dr. Faye: Sure. I'm a medical researcher[3] at Pharmco Labs. I do experiments[4] with animals to find cures for human diseases.

Mr. Bates: I'm Bill Bates. And I'm here as the president of FOA, Friends of Animals. I speak for animal rights.

Moderator: Let's start there. Mr. Bates, what do you mean by animal rights?

Mr. Bates: For me, it means that animals should live in freedom. Humans have rights, and so do animals.

Dr. Faye: Oh, that's ridiculous[5]. Animals have no rights. Humans have always used animals in their daily lives.

Moderator: Okay, now it is obvious[6] that you two don't agree.

Dr. Faye: That's right. It's obvious that the FOA thinks animals have rights. They don't. Animals are animals. That's all. How can animals have rights?

Moderator: Well, Dr. Faye, aren't humans animals?

Dr. Faye: Well, humans and animals are similar. All need to breathe, to eat, and to sleep. But that's it.

Mr. Bates: Oh, give me a break. Come on. We have so much in common[7] with other animals. We

need to give animals the same respect[8] that we give to each other.

Dr. Faye: But Mr. Bates, surely you recognize that there are important differences. We're above the other animals.

Mr. Bates: No, no, no, no, no. That's so arrogant[9] —

Dr. Faye: Let me —

Mr. Bates: — to think that we're above animals. No, no.

Dr. Faye: Look, let — let me finish, Mr. Bates. We have languages, right? We have civilizations[10] —

Mr. Bates: Yeah.

Dr. Faye: We have art. Because of those differences, I feel that other animals can be used by humans. We can use them for food and clothing; we can use them for medical research to help humans live better and longer.

Mr. Bates: You're right that we have additional abilities that animals don't have, but that's exactly why we should protect them. We don't need to hunt them, to capture[11] them and put them in zoos, to eat them. We don't need to hurt them at all. We can develop substitutes[12] for everything that we now use animals for.

Dr. Faye: Animals aren't worth all that trouble. I believe humans need to use other animals for food, clothing, and medical research. In my opinion, we can use other animals for anything we want.

Moderator: Well, we'll have to cut this off now. We will continue this discussion after the break.

1. What does Mr. Bates think about animal rights?

....
....
....

2. What does Dr. Faye think?

....
....
....

Read these three opinions.

James

Humans should not eat animals or use them for research at all.

Carmen

Animals are on the Earth for humans to use.

Ray

Eating and using animals is cruel, but it cannot be helped.

Match the supporting statements with the opinions. Write the numbers in the boxes.
Each opinion has two supporting statements.

supporting statements

1

To save human lives, we need to use animals for medical research.

2

It's unfortunate, but necessary.

3

We don't need to eat meat to be healthy.

4

Humans are superior to all other animals.

5

Animals are living beings; we must respect them.

6

Animals do not have emotions, so we don't need to consider their feelings.

Now compare with a classmate.

Work in a group of three. Ask your partners:
Do you agree with James? Do you agree with Carmen? Do you agree with Ray?
Answer for each person: *I really agree / I agree / I disagree / I really disagree.*

What do you think about animal rights? State your position and support your ideas.
Use new ideas in addition to the ideas above.

Your Position

Supporting Statements

CLARIFYING & EXCHANGING

Now form groups and discuss your position and supporting statements.

If you could talk with an animal, which one would it be? Why? What would you want to know?
Write as many questions as you can:

animal name
....

reasons
....

What would you want to know?
....

Exchange your questions with a classmate.

A Way to Escape

WARM UP
1. At what age do you think it's okay to drink?
2. Do you think drinking is a problem among young people?
3. What would you do if a friend had a drinking problem?

SITUATION 🎧 **A boy is writing a letter to his high school newspaper's advice column. What does he need advice about?**

Dear Sandra,

I'm writing about a friend's "drinking problem." One of the guys I hang out with[1] likes to drink, and I don't think he's an alcoholic[2] or anything, but last weekend I got involved in some trouble, and I need to know what to do.

On the weekend I usually hang out at the mall[3]. You know, some of the guys like to drink beers out in the parking lot. But a couple of times my best friend Dave (not his real name, of course) brought some hard liquor[4]. I don't know where he gets it. And he got pretty drunk. In fact, every time we go out, he gets really drunk.

The real problem is he can't go home if he's been drinking, so he came home with me and crashed[5] in my bedroom. I had to sneak him in[6] without letting my parents know. If we'd been caught, I'm sure that my parents would have called Dave's parents, and that wouldn't be good. Here's the really bad part. Dave's family seems kind of unstable[7]. His parents are always fighting and I can understand why Dave wants to get away. And even probably why he's drinking so much.

Dave told me that if his father ever caught him drinking again, he would go absolutely ballistic[8], if you know what I mean. Plus, I'm afraid my parents would forbid[9] me from seeing Dave anymore. But, I don't want this to happen because we've been buddies[10] since elementary school.

Anyway, last week I told Dave at school he couldn't come stay at my place if he drank. I said my parents were suspicious, and he promised he wasn't going to drink much, but then that night, just like always, he did. He pleaded with me[11] to let him stay at my place, and what am I supposed to do? I mean, he's my buddy. In the end, I let him come over — I couldn't just abandon[12] him. He apologized the next day, like always, and promised it wouldn't happen again. I'm afraid it will, though, and I don't know what to do. Please help.

Sincerely,
Tom (not my real name)

CHECK YOUR UNDERSTANDING

1. What does Dave do when he's with his friends? ....
2. What is Dave's family like? ....
3. What does the writer do to help Dave? ....

POINTS OF VIEW

Read these three opinions.

Trin

He should tell his parents honestly about Dave.

Carla

He shouldn't tell anyone, but should let Dave stay at his place.

Anton

He should talk to Dave's parents.

Match the supporting statements with the opinions. Write the numbers in the boxes.
Each opinion has two supporting statements.

supporting statements

1

Tom needs to find some help for Dave.

2

If Dave is in trouble, Dave's family needs to know about it.

3

Dave may not be telling the truth. His family probably wants to help him.

4

Tom needs to tell the truth about Dave, even if he loses Dave as a friend.

5

Tom is old enough to deal with his own problems. He doesn't need to involve his or Dave's parents.

6

It might be a temporary problem. Tom should wait to see what happens.

Now compare with a classmate.

Work in a group of three. Ask your partners:
Do you agree with Trin? Do you agree with Carla? Do you agree with Anton?
Answer for each person: *I really agree / I agree / I disagree / I really disagree.*

WHAT ARE YOUR VALUES?

Do you think Dave has a serious problem? State your position and support your ideas.
Use new ideas in addition to the ideas above.

Your Position

Supporting Statements

CLARIFYING & EXCHANGING

Now form groups and discuss your position and supporting statements.

DEBATE ACTIVITY   Should alcohol be treated like a drug?

Work in a group. Divide into two teams, "For" and "Against." Write down your ideas. Think about how you will answer the other side's ideas. Debate the question for 10 minutes.

my ideas

....

....

....

useful phrases

Beginning – The way I see it... If you ask me...
Disagreeing – I don't think so... That may be true, but...
Ending – Regardless, I think... In spite of what you say, I think...

Adult Children

WARM UP
1. When should children leave their parents' house?
2. What's good about living with your parents? What's bad?
3. What's good about living by yourself? What's bad?

SITUATION 🎧 *World Trend* is an international talk show about world cultural trends. Today's topic is children who live at home. **What do you learn from the speakers about this topic?**

Moderator: Hello, everybody. Welcome to *World Trend,* your international talk show about young people's trends from around the world. Today's topic is living at home, young adults who live with their parents. Is this a global phenomenon[1]? Let's find out. In the studio we've got Professor Yumi Hasegawa, from Japan, and Dr. William Caldwell, from the U.K. Professor Hasegawa, tell us about Japan.

Professor Hasegawa: Well, in Japan, it is a growing trend. We call an unmarried person who has a job but who still lives with their parents a parasite single[2].

Moderator: "Parasite single"! Wow, that sounds kind of creepy[3]! What about you, Dr. Caldwell, what... what about in the U.K.

Dr. Caldwell: Yes. Well,

recently we've had an increase[4] in the number of children who have left the nest and later return to live with their parents even though they have jobs and earn money. We call them "boomerang children."

Moderator: Boomerang children. Ah, yes. They leave, but then they always come back. So, Professor Hasegawa, it sounds like "parasite singles" are considered a negative thing in Japan? Is that right?

Professor Hasegawa: Well, the word "parasite" isn't very nice, is it? And yes, it is somewhat negative. Many people think that parasite singles are selfish.

Moderator: Oh. Selfish? What do you mean? In what way?

Professor Hasegawa: Well, the stereotype[5] in Japan is that they just want to have fun, and always need their mommy washing their laundry. They don't want any responsibility.

Dr. Caldwell: In most European countries and North America, I believe, the situation is similar. It used to be that young people wanted to leave home to be free. Now, because so many adult children return home, it's often the parents who want some freedom.

Moderator: I bet they do.[6] Interesting! Well, well... is there an upside[7] to any of this?

Professor Hasegawa: The upside? Well, personally, I think that staying at home longer gives children time to think about their future more carefully.

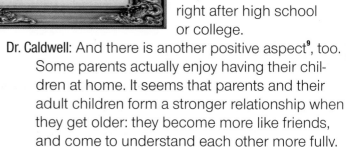

Some parasite singles simply want to make careful choices: for example, they don't want to marry the wrong person or pursue[8] the wrong career, which they might do if they had to leave home right after high school or college.

Dr. Caldwell: And there is another positive aspect[9], too. Some parents actually enjoy having their children at home. It seems that parents and their adult children form a stronger relationship when they get older: they become more like friends, and come to understand each other more fully.

Moderator: Hey — let's see what our listeners have to say about this. Are these people disgusting[10] parasites? Or just careful? Does this happen in your country? Give us a call right now. The number is...

CHECK YOUR UNDERSTANDING

1. What is a parasite single? ....
2. What are boomerang children? ....
3. What are the benefits of adult children living at home?
....
4. What are the disadvantages? ....

Koji

A working adult child living with parents is a good lifestyle choice.

Trin

Adult children who are working should never live with their parents.

James

It's okay for an adult to live at home temporarily, but not for too long.

Match the supporting statements with the opinions. Write the numbers in the boxes.
Each opinion has two supporting statements.

supporting statements

1

Adult children are a lot of trouble for their parents.

2

Adult children can have a high standard of living.

3

After a while, adult children need to create their own families and contribute more to society.

4

It's childish for adults to need someone to take care of them.

5

Living with your parents is more convenient than living alone.

6

If an adult child stays at home permanently, he or she will never grow up.

Now compare with a classmate.

Work in a group of three. Ask your partners:
Do you agree with Koji? Do you agree with Trin? Do you agree with James?
Answer for each person: *I really agree / I agree / I disagree / I really disagree.*

WHAT ARE YOUR VALUES?

Is it okay for working adult children to live with their parents? State your position and support your ideas.
Use new ideas in addition to the ideas above.

Your Position

Supporting Statements

CLARIFYING & EXCHANGING

Now form groups and discuss your position and supporting statements.

VALUES SURVEY

How important are the following lifestyle choices for you? Choose the three most important values for you.

.... Getting married and having children
.... Being able to enjoy my hobbies
.... Being free from my parents
.... Keeping my own schedule
.... Having my own space

.... Being able to enjoy traveling a lot
.... Keeping a high standard of living
.... Staying close to my family
your own value:
....

Compare your answers with a partner. Then compare answers with the class.

Glossary

INTRO UNIT

1. investigate: explore, study
When students *investigate* their personal beliefs, they learn better. = When students *explore* their personal beliefs, they learn better.
2. reluctant: hesitant, shy
Some students are *reluctant to talk about* personal experiences. = Some students *don't feel comfortable talking about* personal experiences.
3. global topics: issues that are important around the world
Students should discuss *important global topics*. = Students should discuss *issues that affect the whole world*.
4. cross-cultural communication: talking to people from other cultures
Impact Values should stress *cross-cultural communication*. = *Impact Values* should stress *interaction among people from many backgrounds*.

UNIT 1

1. weird: strange, unusual
It's actually getting kind of *weird*. = The situation is becoming a little *uncomfortable*.
2. make something last: let something continue
You've got to find a way to *make it last*. = *You need to keep the relationship going*.
3. awesome: great, wonderful, fantastic
Michelle is *awesome*! = Michelle is *really fantastic*.
4. cool: great, wonderful
She got her nose pierced./ *Cool*. = She got her nose pierced./ *That's great*.
5. belly button: navel
Then she got her *belly button* pierced.
6. disgusting: sickening, gross
I did kiss her... It was *disgusting*. = It *made me feel sick*.
7. express yourself: say or show how you feel, say or show how you are
She said it was her right to *express herself*. = She said it was her right to *show her individuality*.
8. turn someone on: excite, stimulate
If *it turns her on*, you should do it. = If *she really likes it*, you should do it.
9. totally: I really agree
I can't believe you agree with her./ *Totally*. = I can't believe you agree with her./ *I completely agree*.

UNIT 2

1. dormitory: a building with rooms for college students
I lived in a *dormitory* my first year.
2. social: outgoing, friendly
A childhood full of television made me *less social*. = A childhood full of television made me *shy*.
3. make up your mind: decide to, be determined to
I *made up my mind* to do better. = I *promised myself* to do better.
4. pop into your head: think of suddenly, without knowing why
Then an idea *popped into my head*. = Then an idea *sprang to mind*.
5. crystal clear: very obvious
Suddenly *it became crystal clear*. = Suddenly *I understood completely*.
6. vow: promise
I have *vowed* that television won't be a major part of my life. = I have *promised* that television won't be a major part of my life.

UNIT 3

1. rugged: handsome in a rough or strong way, muscular, powerful
I prefer a guy to look more natural and *rugged*.
2. masculine: manly, like a typical man
I prefer a guy to look more natural and masculine. = I prefer a guy to look more *traditionally manly*.
3. foundation: skin-colored makeup used as a base
You've got on *foundation* and blush.
4. blush: powder for the cheeks
You've got on foundation and *blush*.
5. social stereotype: a simple, sometimes untrue, belief about a group of people
Who came up with these *social stereotypes*? = Who came up with these *cultural norms*?
6. weird: strange, not normal or natural
Doesn't *that seem weird to you*? = Don't *you think that's odd*?
7. strike you as: seem to you
Doesn't it *strike you as* a little odd... = Don't *you think* it's a little odd...

UNIT 4

1. fixed: changed to look better with surgery, improved
I'm going to get my eyelids *fixed*. = I'm going to get my eyelids *done*.

2. cosmetic surgery: surgery to improve your appearance
You're going to get *cosmetic surgery?*
3. drastic: extreme, much more than is necessary
I'm not going to *do anything drastic.* = I'm not going to *go overboard.*
4. approach: talk to, get to know
I'll be *approached* by more boys. = More boys will *try to get to know me.*
5. attract someone: draw someone's attention to you, make someone notice you
You should *attract people* with your inner beauty. = You should *make people notice you* with your inner beauty.
6. wit: sense of humor
Boys aren't attracted by your intelligence and your *wit.*

Unit 5

1. mention: say casually, happen to say
Sheila *mentioned* she couldn't find a dog-sitter. = Sheila *happened to say* she couldn't find a dog sitter.
2. dog-sitter: someone who takes care of a dog while its owners are away.
Sheila was having trouble finding a *dog-sitter* for Rex. = Sheila was having trouble finding *someone to take care of* Rex.
3. be willing: agree, want to
He was sure I would *be willing* to help. = He was sure I would *want to* help.
4. mind something: dislike, feel bad about doing something
I really didn't mind doing it. = *Doing it wasn't so bad.*
5. my whole day was shot: it took the entire day, it lasted the entire day
It only took 10 minutes to fix the window, but *my whole day was shot.* = It only took 10 minutes to fix the window, but *it ruined my entire day.*

Unit 6

1. cool: great, wonderful
It's so *cool* that she dresses that way. = It's so *great* that she dresses that way.
2. hip: cool, very fashionable
She looks so young and *hip.* = She looks so young and *fashionable.*
3. embarrassing: making someone feel ashamed or self-conscious
My mother is so *embarrassing.*
4. drive someone crazy: make someone upset and frustrated
She's *driving me crazy* with the way she wears young clothes. = She's *driving me nuts* with the way she wears young clothes.
5. bleach: lighten hair to a blond color
She *bleached* her hair.
6. tattoo: a permanent ink design on someone's skin
She says she might get a *tattoo.*
7. go overboard: to be extreme, to go too far
My mom has gone *completely overboard.* = My mom has gone *way too far.*

Unit 7

1. inedible: impossible to eat
She makes these special dishes, but they're *inedible.*
2. klutz: a clumsy, awkward person
He's a *klutz.* = He's *really clumsy.*
3. disaster: a terrible situation
It's such a *disaster!*

Unit 8

1. sensitive: easily hurt
Stanley is kind of shy and *sensitive.*
2. madly in love: feeling passionate love for
He says he's *madly in love with* a woman. = He says he's *crazy about* a woman.
3. weird: strange, not normal or natural
That's a little *weird,* because she's not shy at all. = That's *strange,* because she's not shy at all.
4. be someone's type: be the kind of person someone is usually attracted to
I don't think Stanley *is her type.* = I don't think *she's attracted to* Stanley.
5. overreacting: worrying too much, thinking the situation is more serious than it really is
He told me I was *overreacting.* = He told me I was making a *big deal out of nothing.*
6. direct: straightforward, honest
He's finally being *direct.*
7. employee files: folders or a database with information about a company's employees
He looked at the *employee files.*
8. stalker: someone who secretly follows another person
I think he might be turning into a *stalker.*

Unit 9

1. run late: be late
So what if *she runs late?* = So what if *she's late a lot?*
2. It's not that big a deal: It's not very important.
So what if she runs late? *It's not that big a deal.* = So what if she runs late? *It's not a problem.*
3. disrespect: impoliteness, not taking other people's feelings seriously enough
Being late is a sign of *disrespect.*
4. disorganized: careless, sloppy about planning
She's just *disorganized.* = She's just *not very together.*
5. embarrassing: making someone feel ashamed or self-conscious
It was really *embarrassing.*
6. rude: impolite, inconsiderate
That's *rude* and selfish. = That's *inconsiderate* and selfish.

Unit 10

1. Sweetie: Honey, Darling
Sweetie, do you know what day it is? = *Darling,* do you know what day it is?

2. real busy: very busy
I'm *real busy* right now. = I'm *very busy* right now.
3. agh: an expression of frustration
I'm busy right now./ *Agh!*
4. appointment: meeting time, a set time to see someone
I will send an email to my doctor to make an *appointment*.
5. what is wrong with you?: Why are you behaving this way? I'm worried about you
What is wrong with you? You spend all of your time with your computer. = *What's the matter with you?* You spend all of your time with your computer.
6. checkup: a physical; a general examination
I will see my doctor and get a *checkup*.

Unit 11

1. anniversary: the yearly celebration of something important
Today is our first *anniversary!*
2. let go of: let someone leave, let someone end the relationship
I would not want to *let go of him*. = I wouldn't want to *let him leave*.
3. unrealistic: unreasonable, too demanding
Frank's wife is *being unrealistic*. = Frank's wife is *fooling herself*.
4. figure out: understand what's happening, understand what to do
He still has to *figure out what will happen to* his kids. = He still has to *decide what to do about* his kids.
5. liar: someone who doesn't tell the truth
Virginia says that Frank is a *liar*. = Virginia says that Frank is *dishonest*.
6. cheat on someone: have a secret relationship
Frank has *cheated on his wife*. = Frank has *had an affair*.
7. be unfaithful to someone: have a secret relationship with someone else
Frank has *been unfaithful to his wife*. = Frank has *had an affair*.

Unit 12

1. upset: sad and worried
You look *upset*. = You look *worried*.
2. bossy: trying to tell someone what to do, controlling
He told me that I was being *bossy*. = He told me that I was *telling him what to do*.
3. yell at: shout at, scream at
He *yelled* at me. = He *screamed* at me.
4. slave: someone who is owned by another person, servant
I told him *I wasn't his slave*. = I told him *he didn't own me*.
5. grab: hold tightly
He *grabbed* my arm.
6. break up with: end the relationship
I decided to *break up with* him. = I decided to *end the relationship with* him.
7. shocked: stunned, scared, horrified
I was so *shocked*. = I was so *horrified*.
8. promise: vow, give your word
He *promised* he would stop drinking. = He *gave me his word* he would stop drinking.

Unit 13

1. mean: nasty, not nice
He's *mean* to me. = He's *not nice* to me.
2. harshly: roughly or critically
He *speaks harshly to* me. = He *is critical of* me.
3. criticize: point out someone's faults, find the weak points of something
He *criticizes* my work. = He *tells me* my work *is no good*.
4. employees: workers
He jokes and acts friendly with the other *employees*.
5. terrific: really great, wonderful
The other workers *say he is terrific*. = The other workers *really like him*.
6. reach everyone: contact everyone, speak with everyone personally
I had to *reach* everyone by Monday. = I had to *call* everyone by Monday.
7. set someone up to fail: make it impossible for someone to succeed
My boss is *setting me up to fail*. = My boss is *making it impossible for me to do well*.
8. fire: make someone leave their job, terminate
Your boss is trying to *fire* you.
9. get away with it: do something wrong or unfair without getting caught
Don't let him *get away with it*. = Don't let him *do this to you*.
10. mistreated: treated badly or unfairly
Tell him you feel *you're being mistreated*. = Tell him you feel *he's not treating you right*.
11. go over someone's head: talk to someone higher up in the company
Here, you don't *go over your boss's head*. = Here, you don't *talk to your boss's boss*.
12. continue to try: keep trying
I will *continue to try to do my best*. = I'll *just keep trying*.

Unit 14

1. weird: strange, not normal or natural
My boss is acting *weird*. = My boss is acting *strange*.
2. updating: giving someone the latest news about
I was *updating* him on a project. = I was *letting him know how* the project *was going*.
3. ask someone out: ask someone on a date
My boss *asked me out*. = My boss *asked me on a date*.
4. get it: understand, see the situation
Oh, I *get it*. You don't like him. = Oh, *I see*. You don't like him.
5. like (someone) that way: feel attracted to someone, have romantic feelings for someone
Oh, I get it. *You don't like him that way*. = Oh, I get it. *You're not attracted to him*.
6. inappropriate: wrong for the situation, not proper for the situation
It was just so *inappropriate*. = It was just so *out of line*.
7. creepy: weird, uncomfortable
It was *creepy*. = It made me feel *really uncomfortable*.
8. threaten: promise something bad will happen
Did he *threaten* to fire you?

9. mess everything up: ruin a situation
It's going to *mess everything up.* = It's going to *ruin everything.*
10. come to that: get that bad, become such a big problem
I don't think *it'll come to that.* = I don't think *that will actually happen.*
11. give it a shot: try it and see what happens
Why don't you *give it a shot?* = Why don't you *try it and see what happens?*

Unit 15

1. get along with people: like people, socialize with people, fit in with other people
He was worried about how you were *getting along with everyone.* = He was worried about how you were *fitting in.*
2. hire: give someone a job, employ
We *hired* you because you speak Japanese.
3. official: formally part of the job
We spend time talking about work things... *nothing official,* but it helps. = We spend time talking about work things... *not formally,* but it helps.
4. be pressured: be forced, feel as if you have to do something
I don't want to *be pressured* to go drinking. = I don't want to *feel like I have to go* drinking.
5. get ahead: become successful
That's the only way to *get ahead* here. = That's the only way to *be successful* here.
6. get drunk: drink too much
I don't want to *get drunk* with my boss. = I don't want to *drink too much* with my boss.
7. unprofessional: not appropriate for work, not proper behavior for work
Getting drunk with my boss is *unprofessional.* = It's *inappropriate* to get drunk with my boss.
8. I respect your opinion: It's okay for us to disagree
I respect your opinion. But I don't think that's the way Mr. Tanaka sees it. = *If that's what you think.* But I don't think that's the way Mr. Tanaka sees it.

Unit 16

1. a touchy subject: a sensitive topic, something difficult to talk about
It's kind of *a touchy subject.* = It's kind of *a sensitive issue.*
2. evaluations: surveys students answer about what they think of their teachers
She always gets high *evaluations.*
3. have an argument: fight, have a disagreement
Did you two *have an argument?* = Did you two *have a fight?*
4. distract: take someone's thoughts or attention away from something
It *distracts* the students. = It *makes* the students *lose focus.*
5. indirectly: not in a direct way, without saying something exactly
I tried to bring it up *indirectly.* = I tried to tell her *in a roundabout way.*
6. responsibility: duty or obligation
Don't we have a *responsibility* to the students? = Don't we

owe it to the students?
7. bring it up: mention it, say it
You should *bring it up* at the next teachers meeting. = You should *say something about it* at the next teachers meeting.
8. dress code: rules telling people how to dress
We should recommend a *dress code* at the next teachers' meeting.

Unit 17

1. employee refrigerator: a refrigerator at a company that is used by the staff
I went to the *employee refrigerator* to get my lunch.
2. pretend: act as if you feel or will do one thing, when you really want to do something else
I *pretended* to go for coffee. = I *acted as if* I was going for coffee.
3. might as well do it: it will be okay to do it
I *might as well have* a second piece. = *It will be okay if I have* a second piece.
4. in heaven: delighted, very happy
I was *in heaven* when I ate the chocolate. = I was *very happy* when I ate the chocolate.
5. retie: tie again
I closed the box and *retied* the ribbon.
6. explosion: blowup, disaster
The explosion came the next day. = *Disaster struck* the next day.
7. client: a customer of the company, a person using the company's services
The chocolates were for a *client.*
8. embarrassment: a feeling of being ashamed
My boss *nearly died of embarrassment.* = My boss *was horribly ashamed.*
9. furious: really angry
Our boss is still *furious.* = Our boss is still *really angry.*
10. colleagues: co-workers
My *colleagues* are disgusted with her attitude.
11. disgusted: upset and angry, made sick by
My colleagues are *disgusted* with her attitude. = My colleagues are *sickened by* her attitude.

Unit 18

1. kidding: joking, not being serious
You're kidding, right? = *You can't be serious, can you?*
2. reputation: someone's position or standing with other people, the opinion people have
Wastrix has such a *bad reputation.* = Most people *have a bad opinion* of Wastrix.
3. burn out: stop liking something, get tired of something
You might *burn out.* = You might *hate it after awhile.*
4. give it a shot: try it out, see if it works
I have to at least *give it a shot.* = I have to at least *try it.*
5. competitive atmosphere: feeling that people have to work harder than their colleagues
A lot less overtime, a *less competitive atmosphere.* = A lot less overtime, a *more friendly work environment.*
6. toxic: poisonous
Wastrix makes all those *toxic* chemicals.

7. lawsuit: legal complaint, legal action, complaint against someone through the court
They have all those *lawsuits* about polluting the environment.
8. environmentally friendly: good for the environment
Econotron is a much more *environmentally friendly* company.
9. naive: very innocent, not realistic enough
You're really *being naive.* = You're really *not being realistic.*

Unit 19

1. permanently: forever, indefinitely
Work in the hotel *permanently?* = Work in the hotel *forever?*
2. job opportunity: chance for a good job
I have such better *job opportunities.* = I have better *job prospects.*
3. quit my job: leave my job
I'll have to *quit my job* and just work in the hotel. = I'll have to *leave my job* and work in the hotel.

Unit 20

1. independent: able to take care of yourself, able to do things by yourself
Marcos was old enough to *be more independent.* = Marcos was old enough to *do more things by himself.*
2. child-care center: day care, a place that takes care of children during the day
I put Marcos in a *child-care center.*
3. advertising agency: a company that creates advertising and commercials
I went back to my old job at the *advertising agency.*
4. traditional: conservative, cautious
Raul is so *traditional.* = Raul is so *conservative.*
5. co-workers: colleagues, the people you work with
I like my job and my *co-workers.*
6. exhausted: very tired
When I finally get home after work, I'm *exhausted.* = When I finally get home after work, I'm *so tired.*

Unit 21

1. adopted: raised by people other than my birth parents, raised by another family
You see, I'm *adopted.*
2. traditional: normal, regular, typical, what you would expect
I don't have a *traditional* mother and father. = I don't have a mother and father, *like you'd expect.*
3. gay: homosexual
I was adopted by two men, a *gay* couple.
4. supportive: positive, giving
My parents are really *supportive.* = My parents are really *there for me.*
5. disappointed: sad, upset
My parents aren't *disappointed.* = My parents aren't *upset.*
6. allowed to: permitted to, okay to
He wasn't *allowed* to be friends with me anymore.
7. good influence: a good companion for, good to be around
They said I wasn't a *good influence on* their son. = They said I wasn't *having a good effect on* their son.

8. complain about: accuse, say bad things about
They *complained* about my parents.
9. corrupting: being a bad influence on, making someone a bad person
They said my parents were *corrupting* the kids. = They said my parents *were a bad influence on* the kids.
10. regret: feel sad about something that happened, wish you could have done something differently
I don't *regret* any of the hard times. = I would do it all over again.
11. count on: trust, rely on
I can really *count on* my parents. = My parents *are really trustworthy.*
12. gender: sex, being male or female
Being a good parent has nothing to do with *gender.*

Unit 22

1. in touch with: in contact with, talking or visiting often
You feel strongly about Rozenn *staying in touch* with your family. = You feel strongly about Rozenn *keeping in contact* with your family.
2. crushed: very hurt and upset
My parents would be *crushed* if Rozenn didn't go back. = My parents would be *so disappointed* if Rozenn didn't go back.
3. biculturally: with two cultures
We promised to raise her *biculturally.*
4. lose touch with: lose contact with, stop feeling close to
Rozenn will *lose touch with* Brazil.
5. in the end: eventually, after a time
She'll thank us *in the end.* = She'll thank us *in the long run.*

Unit 23

1. pregnant: going to have a baby
I just found out. Jan is *pregnant.* = I just found out. Jan is *going to have a baby.*
2. abortion: the removal of a fetus (developing baby) to stop a pregnancy
She wants to have an *abortion.*
3. go through with something: decide to do something
She shouldn't *go through with* the abortion. = She shouldn't *have* the abortion.
4. convince: persuade, show someone through giving your opinion
We have to *convince* her to change her mind. = We have to *make* her change her mind.
5. I'm not with you: I don't agree with you
I'm *not with you on this one,* honey. = I *don't see it that way,* honey.
6. ruin: destroy
It'll *ruin* your life. = It'll *wreck* your life.
7. amazing: wonderful, awesome
You were *amazing.* = You were *wonderful.*
8. handle it: do a good job, do everything necessary
You could *handle it.* = You could *do it all.*
9. raise the baby: take care of the baby, be a parent
I was there to help you *raise the baby.* = I was there to help you *take care of the baby.*

10. responsible: dutiful, mature
She's not *responsible* enough to have a baby. = She's not *mature* enough to have a baby.
11. scared: frightened
She's just saying that because she's *scared*. = She's just saying that because she's *frightened*.
12. responsibility: reliability, dependability, doing your duty
Being a mother teaches *responsibility*. = Being a mother teaches *dependability*.

Unit 24

1. motherhood: being a mother
I know how wonderful *motherhood* is.
2. crib: a baby's bed
We had everything ready for him: the *crib,* the clothes...
3. cruel: mean, nasty
We can't even hold him. It's so *cruel*. = We can't even hold him. It's so *mean*.
4. refuse: say no, not be willing
The surrogate mother *refuses to* give us our baby. = The surrogate mother *won't* give us our baby.
5. contract: a written legal agreement
We already signed a *contract*.
6. egg: female reproductive cell, what a woman contributes to create a fetus
It was my *egg* that was fertilized with my husband's sperm.
7. fertilized: made into a fetus (developing baby)
It was my egg that was *fertilized* with my husband's sperm.
8. sperm: male reproductive cell, what a man contributes to create a fetus
It was my egg that was fertilized with my husband's *sperm*.
9. prematurely: before being mature or ready
Brian was born *prematurely*.
10. put (a baby) up for adoption: give a child away to be raised by another family.
I couldn't *put him up for adoption*. = I couldn't *give him away*.
11. afford: be able to pay for
I may not be able to *afford* to keep him. = I may not be able to *make enough money* to keep him.

Unit 25

1. tough: difficult, uncomfortable, hard-hitting
...the interview show with *tough* talk, and *tough* questions. = the interview show with *hard-hitting* talk and *hard-hitting* questions.
2. author: writer
We're with John Sanders, *author* of a controversial new book.
3. controversial: causing conflicts or disagreements
We're with John Sanders, author of a *controversial* new book. = We're with John Sanders, author of a *hotly debated* new book.
4. future generations: people who are going to be born and grow up in the future, generations to come after us
We will be hated by *future generations*. = We will be hated by the *generations to come*.
5. in crisis: in an emergency situation

We're *in crisis,* and it's a result of our selfishness. = We're *in an emergency situation,* and it's a result of our selfishness.
6. consume: use products
We *consume,* we waste, and we think it's all natural.
7. CO_2: carbon dioxide
We produce *CO_2,* which causes global warming.
8. courage: bravery, strength
No one has the *courage* to change. = No one has the *strength* to change.
9. chemical-free: without chemicals
I grow my own *chemical-free* vegetables. = I grow my own *organic* vegetables.
10. public transportation: trains, subways or metros, and buses
I always take *public transportation*.
11. practical: realistic, convenient
That's *not practical*. = That's *not realistic*.
12. available: for sale
It's *available* in every bookstore.

Unit 26

1. tenant: renter
She's a great *tenant*.
2. limitation: weakness, what someone can and can't do safely
She knows *her limitations* now. = She knows *what she can and can't do* now.
3. lease is coming up for renewal: the apartment can be legally rented to someone else
The *lease is coming up for renewal* next month. = The *contract is up* next month.
4. nursing home: a home for elderly people who need some medical care
Well, then put her in a *nursing home*.
5. responsibility: duty, obligation,
She's your *responsibility,* not mine. = She's your *duty,* not mine.

Unit 27

1. confused: having a hard time understanding
I'm *confused* these days. = I'm *mixed up* these days.
2. violence: hurting someone physically
We are taught that *violence* is bad. = We are taught that *hurting people* is bad.
3. come to an agreement: work something out, decide the situation
I should talk with my friend, and *come to an agreement*. = I should talk with my friend, and *figure out a solution*.
4. civilized: polite, peaceful, educated
Violence is the least *civilized* way to solve problems. = Violence is the least *educated* way to solve problems.
5. injured: hurt
If one *injured* the other, they would be arrested. = If one *harmed* the other, they would be arrested.
6. arrest: to have the police capture someone
If one injured the other, they would be *arrested*.
7. murder: kill someone on purpose

If one killed the other, it would be a *murder*.

8. refugees: people who have been made homeless by war
And wars create *refugees,* too.

9. extreme: much more than is neccessary, going too far
A war is *extreme* violence. = A war is *the worst level of* violence.

10. wisdom: intelligence
Why can't they *use their wisdom* and talk it over? = Why can't they talk it over *intelligently?*

11. contradict: disagree with, say the opposite of
Why are they *contradicting* themselves? = Why are they *saying one thing and doing another?*

Unit 28

1. animal rights: treating animals with fairness and kindness
Today's program is about *Animal Rights*.

2. perspective: point of view, way of thinking
We have two guests here to challenge our perspective. = We have two guests here to challenge our *way of thinking*.

3. researcher: a person who does research
I'm a medical *researcher* at Pharmco Labs.

4. do experiments: to perform scientific research
I *do experiments with* animals. = I *do research on* animals.

5. ridiculous: laughable, stupid
Oh, that's *ridiculous*. = Oh, that's *just stupid*.

6. obvious: easy to see or understand
It's *obvious* that you don't agree. = It's *clear* that you don't agree.

7. have so much in common: are the same in many ways
We *have so much in common* with other animals. = We *are so similar to* other animals.

8. respect: seriousness about someone's worth or importance
We need to *give animals the same respect* we give each other. = We need to *treat animals with the same fairness and dignity* that we treat each other.

9. arrogant: thinking you are too important or better
We are above the other animals./ That's so *arrogant*. = We are above the other animals./ That's so *superior*.

10. civilizations: complex, intelligent cultures
We have languages, we have *civilizations*.

11. capture: catch, take
We don't need to hunt or *capture* animals. = We don't need to hunt or *catch* animals.

12. substitutes: replacements, other useful things
We can develop *subsitutes* for everything we now use animals for. = We can develop *replacements* for everything we now use animals for.

Unit 29

1. hang out with: spend time with
A guy I hang out with likes to drink. = *One of my friends* likes to drink.

2. alcoholic: someone who can't control his or her drinking
I don't think he's an *alcoholic*. = I don't think he's a *problem drinker*.

3. mall: shopping center
I usually hang out at the *mall*.

4. hard liquor: a drink with a lot of alcohol, such as whiskey
My friend Dave brought some *hard liquor*.

5. crash: (slang) sleep
He *crashed* in my bedroom. = He *slept over* in my bedroom.

6. sneak him in: take him inside *secretly*
I had to *sneak him into* my house. = I had to *bring him inside* my house secretly.

7. unstable: in an uncertain situation, not calm or steady
Dave's family seems kind of *unstable*. = Dave's family seems kind of *unsteady*.

8. go ballistic: (slang) get really angry, become out of control
If he caught Dave drinking, he would *go* absolutely *ballistic*. = If he caught Dave drinking, he would *go crazy*.

9. forbid: say someone can't do something, not allow
My parents would *forbid me* from seeing Dave anymore. = My parents *wouldn't allow me to* see Dave anymore.

10. buddy: friend
We've been *buddies* since elementary school. = We've been *friends* since elementary school.

11. plead: beg, ask strongly
He *pleaded with me* to let him stay. = He *begged me* to let him stay.

12. abandon: leave
I couldn't just *abandon him*. = I couldn't just *leave him there*.

Unit 30

1. global phenomenon: something that happens all over the world
Is this a *global phenomenon?* = Is this a *worldwide trend?*

2. parasite single: (a term that originated in Japan) a person who lives with his or her parents while working.
We call an unmarried person who has a job but who still lives with their parents a *parasite single*.

3. creepy: weird, strange, unnatural
That sounds kind of *creepy*. = That sounds kind of *weird*.

4. increase: growth, rise
We've had an *increase* in the number of adult children who live with their parents. = We've had a *rise* in the number of adult children who live with their parents

5. stereotype: a simplistic, sometimes untrue, belief about a group of people
The *stereotype* is that they just want to have fun.

6. bet they do: that makes sense, that seems reasonable
It's often the parents who want some freedom./ *I bet they do*. = It's often the parents who want some freedom./ *That makes a lot of sense*.

7. upside: positive or good things
Is there an *upside* to any of this? = Is there *any good* to any of this?

8. pursue: follow, keep trying
They don't want to *pursue the wrong career*. = They don't want to *follow the wrong career path*.

9. positive aspect: upside, a good thing
There is another *positive aspect,* too. = There is another *benefit,* too.

10. disgusting: gross, unnatural, creepy
Are these people *disgusting* parasites? = Are these people *gross* parasites?

Extension Activities

FOCUSED SKILL DEVELOPMENT

You may wish to help your students develop specific language skills as they work with *Impact Values*. In this section, you will find a range of activities that can be adapted to any unit in *Impact Values*.

(SPEAKING)

1. Read and Look Up

Choose a unit with a conversation (not a monologue). Place students in pairs or groups, depending on the number of speakers. Have them choose one of the speakers. Students read silently and then look up and repeat what they've read. Make sure that the students look at each other when talking. Have them change roles when they have done the conversation two or three times.

2. Cued Conversation

Select a unit that has a conversation. Place students in pairs. Give each student an index card. Each student makes a short summary of the lines of his or her character on the index card. Provide a five-minute time limit for this.

Instruct the students to close their books and use the summaries on their cards as cues to make similar conversations in their own words. As an alternative, students could exchange cards, and use their partners' summaries to make up conversations.

3. Speaking with Emotion

Students work in pairs or groups and read the unit's story or conversation aloud using pace, volume, and intonation to convey one particular emotion (for example, anger or depression). Or, if the story has a conversation, they decide on a different emotion for each character. The others in their group must guess what emotion they are trying to convey.

4. Circle Discussion

Place students in a circle (or, for large classes, make two or three circles). Begin the discussion by giving your opinion about the topic of the unit that you are studying. The student sitting to your right (or left) continues by saying something else about the topic. When that student has finished speaking, it is the next student's turn. Go around the circle until everyone has had an opportunity to say at least one sentence about the topic. Continue by having the students, in reverse order, ask questions about something the previous speaker has said. You might want to start this part of the activity yourself, by asking a question of the student who just finished speaking.

5. Oral Reading

For units that have conversations, students could choose a character and take turns reading to each other. After each line of dialogue, the partner who is listening provides feedback on the reader's intonation and pronunciation.

6. Role Play

Have the students work in pairs or small groups. Assign each person a "role" of one of the characters in the story. The "role" should state what the person is trying to accomplish in the conversation (for example, try to convince Ayu not to have cosmetic surgery). Give the groups a chance to "act out" their roles in the form of a spontaneous conversation.

Here are some considerations when using role plays in language classes:

In setting up a role play, it is important to consider these elements:
• the language the students need to carry out the role play
• the knowledge the students have of the content or subject of the role play
• the setting or the situation of the role play

The activities in each unit of *Impact Values* give the students sufficient practice in the language and provide them with the knowledge needed to successfully complete a role play. This leaves us with the third element in a role play, its setting.

The plausibility of the setting and the content are major considerations. Are the students playing roles that are plausible in terms of both their lives and the content? If the answer is yes to both aspects, then the chances are excellent that the students will be interested in the role play and that it will probably be successful.

During a role play, generally the best thing for the teacher to do is stand back and let the students play their roles. You should observe, of course, but try to avoid interfering. If you intervene, the role play stops. If this happens, you might want to start the role play from the beginning.

Depending on the needs and interests of the students, you could pay attention to mistakes that the students make. Mistakes include factual errors, linguistic errors that cause communication problems, and cultural or social errors in using the language (e.g., formal speech when informal speech is more appropriate). Wait until the role play activity is completed before providing feedback.

You might want to have a debriefing in which students assess the success or failure of the activity. What worked? What didn't go over so well? The feedback that the students provide can be useful in developing the next role play.

Finally, after your students and you have successfully engaged in several role plays, you could ask the students to join you in developing future role plays. You might be pleasantly surprised at how motivated students get when they are actively involved in their own learning.

7. Speeches and Debates

You might want to have students prepare short speeches about the unit topic, or organize the class for a structured debate. For ideas on how to maximize the learning value of speeches and debates, see the section below on Giving Short Speeches and Conducting Debates.

LISTENING

1. Jigsaw Team Comprehension Question

Divide the class into two groups. Give each group a CD player and have them listen to the text two or three times. The first group listens to only the first half of the passage; the second group listens to the second half. Each group prepares four or five comprehension questions on their half of the text.

The groups exchange questions. Each group listens to the other half of the text and answers the questions.

If your class is large, divide the students into small groups.

2. Making Questions

On the board write the answers to four to five comprehension questions that can be answered by listening to the story. Tell the students that they must write the questions for these answers. Play the CD once. Students work in pairs and write their questions. Play the CD a second time and have them go over their questions.

3. Catch the Mistakes

Write a summary of the story on the board (or use an overhead projector). Include in the summary a number of mistakes. Have the students listen to the CD, find the mistakes in the summary, and correct them.

4. Predicting

Use a unit with a conversation. With books closed, play the CD and stop the conversation at key points. Ask the students to work with a partner and predict what they think the next speaker will say. The first few times you do this activity, you could give the students three or four choices. Students select which one they think the next speaker will use. For units with a single speaker, stop the CD at key points and ask the students what the speaker will talk about next. Again, you may wish to give the students some choices.

5. What's Missing?

Using a unit with a conversation, reproduce the conversation but replace all of the lines of one of the speakers with blank lines (e.g., Roy: _____). With books closed, students fill in the blanks with their own ideas. Play the CD and have students compare what they have written with what's on the CD. For other units, reproduce the passage with the key ideas omitted. Then play the CD, and have students compare their written version with the CD.

READING

1. Fill in the Blanks

Retype the story, and replace important or key words with numbered blanks. Students read the story and, working individually or in pairs, fill in the blanks using a list of the missing words.

2. Team Comprehension Questions

Students read through the story, working in pairs or small groups, and write two or three comprehension questions. At first, you will need to specify the type of questions: True/ False, Yes/ No, or WH- information questions. The students exchange their questions with another pair or group and see who can answer them without looking again at the reading.

3. Making Questions

On the board, write four or five answers to questions that can be answered by reading the story. Tell the students that they must write questions for the answers. Students read the story once, then, working alone or in pairs, write their questions. Play the CD as the students follow in their books and have them go over their questions.

4. Order! Order!

Retype the entire story on a piece of paper. Number each sentence, but mix up the ordering of the sentences. Students, in pairs or small groups, put the sentences in the correct order.

A variation is retyping the story with mixed-up paragraphs. The students' job is to put the paragraphs in the correct order. You might want to do this before you do the sentence reordering version, since it is easier.

5. Read and Draw

After the students have read the story, have them individually draw a picture of some aspect of the story.

6. Scanning

Scanning is a good activity to help students develop fluency in reading. Find three or four words (or phrases) that occur frequently in a story. Write them on the board. Have the students read the story as quickly as possible—scan—and count the number of times that the first word occurs. Then do the second word, and so on.

7. Find the Differences

Rewrite the story, changing key words. The

students' job is to compare the two stories and find the differences between the two versions. This can be done as pair work.

VOCABULARY

1. Vocabulary Log

Students keep a vocabulary log in groups or as a class. They can use words and expressions from the glossary, or additional words that come up during classroom activities. Students can take turns being the group vocabulary monitor. The job of the group vocabulary monitor is to write down new or unfamiliar words from a unit on a group list. Every four to six units, collect the lists and give a brief quiz on vocabulary from the lists.

2. Synonyms

Replace glossed words and expressions from a passage with synonyms or similar expressions. Underline the synonyms, and list the original words and expressions (out of order) at the bottom of the page. Ask students to choose replacement words for the synonyms from the bottom of the page and give a reason. Then they compare their choices with what appears in the text.

3. Choose the Translation

You can do this activity if all of the students have the same first language. Look over the story and select words or phrases that might be difficult for or unknown to your students. Translate the words or phrases into the students' first language. Put the translations in random order in one column and the English in a second column. The students, working alone or in pairs, match the translations with their English equivalents.

4. Choose the Definition

Look over the story and select words or phrases that might be difficult or unknown to the students. Define the words or phrases in English. Put the definitions in random order in one column and the words or phrases in a second column. The students, working alone or in pairs, match the definitions with the words or phrases.

WRITING

In-Class Writing

For any of the speaking activities in *Impact Values* — *Warm Up, Check Your Understanding, Points of View, What Are Your Values?* — you can have the students write out their responses first, before they interact orally. This will help students focus on accuracy of vocabulary and grammar. As the students are preparing written responses, you can walk around the class to help with language clarity.

Homework Writing

Teachers often discover that they don't have enough time in class to do all that they want to do. Homework can be used to extend the students' learning in a variety of ways:

- It can be used as a review of material covered in the class.
- It can be used to help the students learn additional information, beyond what was learned in the class.
- It can be used to recycle previously learned material in different formats and contexts.
- It can be used as a way to help students develop long-term learning strategies.

Homework, then, can play an important role in consolidating materials previously learned and in learning new material.

Here are some writing-based activities that you can assign to your students as homework:

1. Journals

Students keep a loose-leaf notebook with a single page entry per class. They can write on the unit topic or on anything that is relevant or of interest to them. The focus is on fluency, not on accuracy, as this is the students' opportunity to communicate directly with you in English. You can collect the journals at the beginning of class, and read and write brief comments. If there is time, return the journals at the end of class; if not, they can be returned in the next class.

2. Proxy Writing

Students write directly to one of the characters in the *Point of View* activity. Alternatively, they could take on the role of the characters from the text and write a conversation, letter, or diary entry from that person's perspective.

3. Making Predictions

Students write a two-paragraph prediction of what will happen to the characters in the *Situation* section.

4. Writing Summaries

After participating in the *Clarifying and Exchanging* activity, students can write a summary of the presentation material or a summary of their group discussion. They then share their summaries with other students for comments.

5. Expanding the Topic

Students listen to the news in their native language or in English to see if they can find a story related to the topic of the unit. Using their own words, they write a description of the story, and explain why they find it interesting. Alternatively, students write about a news article from a newspaper, a magazine, or a website. (See www.impactseries.com/values for ideas.)

6. Making a Collage

Students put together a collage based on their reactions to a topic. They can use photos, pictures, articles, or other materials. You can ask the students to prepare a short written description for you to clarify what they are trying to express. Students bring their collages to class and explain what they mean. Alternatively, put students into groups. Group members guess who made each collage and try to explain it themselves.

7. Vocabulary Notebook

Students keep a vocabulary notebook, with three to seven new words learned in class that day. For homework they write a short passage that uses the new words.

8. Letters to the Editor

If a topic is of particular interest to your students, ask them to write letters to the editor of an English newspaper. Have students bring English-language newspapers to class and, in pairs or small groups, look over letters to the editor. Go over features such as format and length. Then have the students write their own letters as homework. In the next class, students read their letters in small groups. If the students wish to, they can mail their letters to the newspaper.

9. Letters to the Authors

Students write to the authors of *Impact Values*. Students could write about any aspect of a unit, from the topic itself (e.g., This topic is important to me because...) to the opinions of any or all of the three persons in the *Points of View* activity. Students can contact the authors c/o Longman ELT, by email: rday@hawaii.edu, or through the *Impact Values* website: www.impactseries.com/values

Giving Short Speeches and Conducting Debates

One way to help students improve their speaking skills is by having them give short speeches and participate in debates in class. *Impact Values* provides an excellent starting place to help students develop the confidence and the organizational skills that are the foundation of effective communication. Following are some speech- and debate-related activities that will help your students develop these skills.

Short Speeches

Preparing a Speech

Most of us are afraid of speaking in public, even in our first language, and speaking in a foreign language makes us even more nervous. Therefore, students will need help in preparing what to say in their speeches. Here are some tips that you can share with your students to help them prepare:

❶ Choose your topic carefully and make sure you have something interesting to say about it.
Brainstorm ideas on your topic in advance. Choose only two or three key ideas and examples, and order them so that they are easy to understand.
❷ Organize your speech into a beginning, a middle, and an end:
- Beginning: Introduce yourself and your topic. Then say what you are going to talk about and why.
- Middle: Talk about the main points and use examples to explain each one.
- End: Repeat the main ideas in different words and thank your listeners.

Performance Tips

How your students speak is often as important as what they say. Here are some general tips that you can share with your students to help them improve their performance skills:

❶ Remember to stand naturally, face your audience, and make eye contact with people as you speak.
❷ Speak in a strong voice so that everyone can hear you.
❸ Use clear, simple language that everyone can understand.
❹ Change your speaking speed and intonation to emphasize important points and add interest to your speech. Don't worry about making mistakes. Focus on communicating ideas.
❺ Use facial expressions and gestures to illustrate or emphasize key information.

Speech Scripts and Outlines

Some students may want to memorize or read their speech word-for-word from a prepared script. Many teachers feel that this gives less natural speaking and listening practice. To encourage students to be more spontaneous, give them practice preparing a speech outline. A simple outline can consist of (1) the first few sentences of the speech written word for word, to get the students started, (2) a list of key points that the student wants to talk about, (3) the final sentence of the speech written word for word. Students can practice writing key points by beginning with the idea that they want to express and then crossing out any words they feel they can easily remember.

Speech Activities
1. One-Minute Speech

Students sit in small groups and take turns giving one-minute impromptu speeches on the unit topic or about a controversial statement in the *Points of View* activity. You can increase this to two- or three-minute speeches if your students are comfortable with that. Each listener in the group must ask at least one question about something in the speech. This helps students to think on their feet as well as to be better listeners.

2. Short Experience Speech

Students retell a story from the book or something similar that happened in their own lives or to someone they know, using chronological order. Each listener should fill out a short "speech assessment" form (see page 93) or prepare a question to ask the speaker at the end of the story. This will help students to stay involved in the activity and think critically about what makes a good speech.

3. Short Opinion Speech

Students choose an opinion from the *Points of View* activity, and give a one- or two-minute speech on whether they agree or disagree with it and the reasons why they feel that way. They should summarize their main points in the conclusion of their speech.

CONDUCTING DEBATES

A debate presents two opinions on a topic. The speakers try to persuade the listeners that their opinions are correct. One speaker is always *for* the topic (in the *affirmative* position) and the other is *against* it (in the *negative* position). The affirmative speaker begins and explains the topic and the reasons why he or she is in favor of it. Next, it is the negative speaker's turn. First, he or she gives reasons for disagreeing with the topic. Then he or she explains why the affirmative speaker is wrong. Then it is the affirmative speaker's turn again (the *rebuttal*). He or she has the opportunity to explain why his or her position is correct and why the negative speaker's position is wrong. Finally, each speaker gives a short summary of his or her main points.

In order for students to benefit from debates in English and develop their ability to think and express themselves, it is important that everyone tries to say as much as possible in English. To keep the debate activities in English, you will need to go slowly and repeat frequently so that everyone can follow the ideas. Also, be sure to praise students whenever they successfully communicate their ideas in English.

Preparing a Debate

Remind your students they must take a clear stand on the issue. Even if your students don't really believe the stands they are taking, they can still conduct a successful debate.

Here are some ideas you can share with your students to help ensure that their position is clear:

- List points and examples that support your side of the argument.
- Make sure every point you mention is true and important for your case.
- Only mention the opposite viewpoint to show the problems with it.
- Always summarize your points.

Debate Activities

You can use the opinions listed in the *Points of View* activities as bases for debates. However, your students may still need some help practicing the skills they need to form an argument. Here are some activities to help them build their skills:

1. Building Arguments

Choose a statement from the *Points of View* activity. Put the students in small groups and give them four or five minutes to brainstorm reasons why they could agree or disagree with the statement. They should come up with as many reasons as they can, and write them down. Then the students form pairs and choose who will be for or against the statement. They read their reasons and explain them.

2. Refuting Arguments

In small groups, students choose a statement from the *Points of View* activity. Student 1 reads the statement. Student 2 must disagree and give a reason. (You may need to provide some sample sentences for the students to use,

such as *You have a point, however...*) Student 3 must disagree with Student 2 and so on, until they can't think of any more reasons to disagree. Then begin a new topic.

3. Distinguishing Relevant Supporting Information

Choose a topic (for example, abortion), and have students list everything they know about it in five minutes. Then take a clear stand on the topic. (For example, "Abortion is murder.") Students look at their lists and work in pairs to decide which information is relevant and why. They then form new pairs and compare their information.

4. Summarizing

Students work in pairs and take turns giving impromptu two-minute speeches on a strong stand chosen by themselves or by their teacher. After listening to their partner, they must give a one-sentence summary of their partner's argument.

SPEECH/DEBATE ASSESSMENT FORM

Students can use this form to evaluate their classmates' speeches and to provide feedback to help improve their classmates' performance. Make one copy for each student. Students should fill out the form AFTER their classmate has finished speaking.

Your Name: ....

Date: ....

Speech/Debate Title: ....

Name(s) of Speaker(s): ....

Student Performance	Rating	Notes
DELIVERY (speaking speed and volume, eye contact, gestures)		
CONTENT (explanations and examples are easy to understand)		
ORGANIZATION (contains a beginning, a middle, and an end)		

Suggested rating key:
+ = very good   ÷ = okay   – = needs improvement

Notes

Notes

Welcome to the *Impact* Series

■ Coursebooks

■ Conversation courses

■ Skills courses

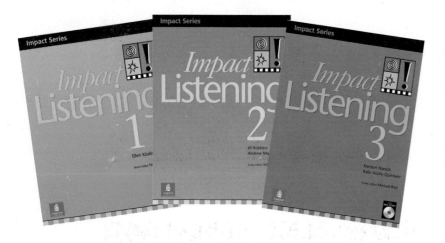

Visit our website for more ideas and teacher discussion.
www.impactseries.com